YORK NOTES

General Editors: Professor A.N. Jeffares (*University of Stirling*) & Professor Suheil Bushrui (*American University of Beirut*)

D1585429

...ce

THE RAINBOW

Notes by Hilda Spear

MA (LONDON) PHD (LEICESTER) FIBA
Lecturer in English, University of Dundee

LONGMAN
YORK PRESS

YORK PRESS
Immeuble Esseily, Place Riad Solh, Beirut.

LONGMAN GROUP LIMITED
London
*Associated companies, branches and representatives
throughout the world*

© Librairie du Liban 1980

First published 1980
Second impression 1986
ISBN 0 582 78191 4

Produced by Longman Group (FE) Ltd
Printed in Hong Kong

Contents

Part 1: Introduction *page* 5

    A note on the text 11

Part 2: Summaries 12

    A general summary 12

    Detailed summaries 15

Part 3: Commentary 37

    The novel as family chronicle 37

    The Bible, the Church and *The Rainbow* 44

    The Rainbow and education 49

    The style of *The Rainbow* 52

Part 4: Hints for study 55

    Model answers 59

Part 5: Suggestions for further reading 63

The author of these notes 65

Part 1

Introduction

D. H. LAWRENCE WAS BORN on 11 September 1885 in Eastwood, a small mining village then about eight miles from Nottingham in the industrial Midlands of England. He was the third son and the fourth child of a marriage which had begun with the magnetism of strong physical passion, but had swiftly deteriorated into a match of incompatibility, indifference and violence.

Lawrence's father, Arthur, was a coal-miner, a 'butty', who organised his own 'butty-gang' of miners and negotiated with the mine owners for their work and pay. A handsome and physically attractive man, full of animal vitality, he was uncultivated, ill-educated and a direct contrast to his wife, Lydia. She was intelligent, cultured, and of a puritanical turn of mind. The marriage seemed doomed to failure almost from the start. Mrs Lawrence soon came to loathe the pit dirt, her husband's excessive drinking and the fellowships in which she had no part; he, in his turn, disliked her finicking ways and constant air of superiority, and became, as time went on, more rather than less boorish. Yet her influence in the family was more powerful than his and one by one the children turned away from their father.

The birth of the fourth child marked a turning-point in their already damaged relationship. Writing to Rachel Annand Taylor just before his mother's death the novelist described his parents' marriage as 'one carnal, bloody fight' and went on to say,

> I was born hating my father: as early as ever I can remember, I shivered with horror when he touched me. He was very bad before I was born.*

The close and stifling relationship with his mother, which coloured the whole of Lawrence's life until her death, grew out of this early sense of fear and hatred of his father, instilled in the child from birth.

The mother took a dominant role in her children's upbringing, encouraging them to despise their father's working-class background and life in the pits and to aspire to a more genteel, middle-class livelihood. She was a devout member of the Congregational Church and the children attended chapel three times every Sunday. Lawrence was brought up on the Bible which he heard read at home, at school and

---

*The Collected Letters of D. H. Lawrence, edited by Harry T. Moore, Heinemann, London, 1962, p. 69.

in the chapel, and the words of the Authorised Version were as familiar to him as the nursery rhymes and fairy tales of his infancy.

However incompatible the marriage partners, the children of the marriage were intelligent and successful. The oldest boy, George, solid and dependable, became an engineer whilst the second brother Ernest was brilliant, mercurial and seemed set for a dazzling career. It was on him that William in *Sons and Lovers* (1913) was moulded and, like William, Ernest suffered an early and untimely death, all his bright promise dissipated. The youngest boy, David Herbert, familiarly known as 'Bertie', became the novelist. Of the two girls in the family, the younger, Ada, was Lawrence's favourite and in the year following his death she published, with the assistance of G. Stuart Gelder, a memoir of his early life.

Lawrence was educated at the local board-school until he was thirteen; then, in 1898, he won a scholarship to Nottingham High School which he attended for the next three years, travelling into Nottingham every day. It was during his last year at school that he first met Jessie Chambers, later to be immortalised and, as she thought, cruelly characterised, as Miriam in *Sons and Lovers.* The Haggs, the Chambers' farmhouse, became a second home to Lawrence. He loved Jessie's kindly and undemanding mother and he loved too the fresh, unspoilt manliness of her father and brothers. The farm was a place to unwind from the tensions of home. With Jessie herself he maintained a strange, involved friendship, part love, part dependence, and Jessie, because she cared for him, endured agonies through his thoughtlessness, his changeability and his withholding of an essential part of himself, some ultimate communion of love which he had reserved for his mother alone. The uncertainties and tortures of his relationship with Jessie are told, from his own point of view, in *Sons and Lovers,* the publication of which in 1913 finally put an end to any possibility of reconciliation between the two.

When Lawrence left school in 1901 he took a position as junior clerk with a firm of surgical goods manufacturers in Nottingham, but soon after this his gifted brother Ernest died, rather suddenly, and Lawrence himself was stricken with pneumonia. He was compelled to leave his work and during the ensuing months he was slowly and lovingly nursed back to health by his distraught mother. After this illness it was decided that he should not return to his job in Nottingham and in the autumn of 1902 he started work as a pupil-teacher. Untrained, and in the lowliest of positions, he found teaching not merely onerous, but often distasteful. The following year, however, he was able to start training at a teacher training centre in Ilkeston, a small town to the south of Eastwood, midway between Nottingham and Derby. With him to the training centre went a number of his friends, Jessie Chambers and her brother

Alan, George Neville and Louie Burrows to whom Lawrence was later to become briefly engaged. Together they formed the core of a closely knit group which came to be known as the 'Pagans'.

From Ilkeston, after a brief period working as an uncertificated teacher, Lawrence went on to the University of Nottingham, intending to read for a degree, but during his first year he transferred to the teacher's certificate course which he completed in 1908. Ursula's teaching and university experiences in *The Rainbow* (1915) are modelled on this period of Lawrence's life.

During all this time he was very close to Jessie Chambers and their warm friendship developed through their common interests; however, urged on by his mother and older sister Emily, Lawrence gradually weaned himself from Jessie's love and when, after his time at university, he took a teaching post in Croydon, he effected his first break with her, though he was still desperately anxious to retain her intellectual companionship. By now he had started writing and Jessie seemed to be necessary to his creative genius. He was writing poetry, short stories, a play and the first draft of *The White Peacock* (1911). All were shown to Jessie for her discussion and approval.

Yet his love for his mother was the most precious part of his life and she was supreme in his affections. By the beginning of his second teaching year in Croydon she had been taken ill with what was, in fact, to prove her terminal illness. Practically every weekend he returned to Eastwood to see her, suffering both for her pain and for himself. Then, when her death was very near, on the spur of the moment and in a railway carriage with several other people present, he proposed to Louie Burrows and was accepted. It was without doubt a reaction to the imminent loss of his mother, a subconscious attempt to appease his own grief. Writing that evening to Rachel Annand Taylor he commented:

> Nobody can have the soul of me. My mother has had it, and nobody can have it again. Nobody can come into my very self again, and breathe me like an atmosphere . . . Louie . . . loves me – but it is a fine, warm, healthy, natural love . . .*

However, he was never to marry her.

A week later, on 9 December 1910, Mrs Lawrence died of cancer. Before his mother's death Lawrence was able to show her a pre-print of *The White Peacock*. The novel was published a month later, in January 1911. The strains which the young novelist had passed through during the previous year helped to contribute to a serious illness towards the end of 1911 and in November he gave up teaching. He now decided to go to Germany as a university lecturer; and to further this ambition he went to visit his former lecturer in French, Professor Ernest Weekley of the

*The Collected Letters of D. H. Lawrence, p. 70.

University of Nottingham. There he fell in love with Professor Weekley's German wife, Frieda. '. . . she's the finest woman I've ever met', he was soon raving to Edward Garnett, 'you must above all things meet her . . . she's splendid, she is really'.* Early in May 1912 they went to Germany together, Frieda leaving her husband and three children behind. A period of uncertainty and anxiety followed before he and Frieda went to Italy and settled down in a village beside Lake Garda. There he worked on *Sons and Lovers* which he had already begun to write before leaving England. It was published in May 1913.

The following year Frieda was divorced, and towards the end of June she and Lawrence returned to London where they were married on 15 July 1914. With the outbreak of war on 4 August they were unable to return to Italy. They remained in England, moving first to Chesham, then to Greatham in Sussex before finally settling down in a cottage on the north Cornish coast. The war created a number of problems in their lives: first, Frieda was, of course, German and came from a distinguished German family; not only this, but she was related to the Von Richthofen brothers, the famous German air aces of the Great War; finally, she frequently made pro-German pronouncements, and Lawrence, who was against the war, became very involved. Their personal life was also very disturbed; bitter and violent quarrels began to develop between them; sometimes these were witnessed by their friends who were horrified but helpless; sometimes the friends were drawn into them, or Lawrence would extend the quarrel to include others. A streak of malice complicated all his relationships, particularly those with women, and a number of his friendships would end with carefully calculated attacks designed by him to hurt and dismay.

Meanwhile, *The Rainbow* had been begun. Lawrence drew his material for it not only from his teaching experiences, but also to some extent from his early relationship with Frieda. Originally called by him *The Sisters*, the novel gave him considerable difficulty. It contained at first material which was later to be cut out of *The Rainbow* and put into its sequel, *Women in Love* (1920). It was not until January 1915 that he took the decision to split his manuscript into two and make two separate novels out of it. *The Rainbow* was finally published in September 1915; in November it was suppressed for alleged indecency. Nevertheless, he pressed on with *Women in Love* and by late October 1916 he was able to write to his agent, J. B. Pinker,

> I have very, very nearly finished – only the concluding chapter to do . . . It is a terrible and horrible and wonderful novel. You will hate it and nobody will publish it.†

*The Collected Letters of D. H. Lawrence, p. 108.
†*The Collected Letters of D. H. Lawrence*, p. 479.

He was right! The novel remained unpublished until late 1920 when it was privately published in New York.

By that time the war was over. Lawrence had been expelled from Cornwall in October 1917, suspected of spying for the Germans, and as soon after the war as was possible he left for the Continent. During the three years after the war he lived mainly in various parts of Italy and then, in 1922, he set off round the world, visiting Ceylon and Australia on his way to America. He made a brief attempt to put down roots in Taos, New Mexico, but he lived a constantly restless and unsettled life, travelling to Mexico and back and forth to Europe, until after a severe illness in 1925 he decided to return permanently to Europe, living mainly in Italy and the south of France.

He was now well established as a writer, publishing not only poems, short stories and novels, but also travel books, critical works and philosophy. The miner's son had come a long way since his first tentative attempts at publication. However, despite his later fame, he was always desperately short of money, pleading with his agent for advances from publishers, and not infrequently begging from his wealthier acquaintances. He never threw off the stigma of immorality in his works and in 1928 his novel *Lady Chatterley's Lover* had to be published in Italy. When copies were smuggled into England, though ostensibly to subscribers only, there was a storm of protest. The following year Lawrence suffered further setbacks. First, the manuscript of his volume of poems, *Pansies*, was seized in the post and when the book came out in July it was published without fourteen of the original poems; secondly, an exhibition of Lawrence's paintings at the Warren Gallery in London was raided by the police and thirteen of the pictures were seized as being 'obscene'. For Lawrence it was a very worrying time and he was becoming increasingly ill with tuberculosis. Early in 1930 he entered a sanatorium in Vence, southern France, but nothing could be done for him and he found the place distressing, writing to Maria Huxley:

> I am rather worse here – such bad nights, and cough, and heart and pain decidedly worse here – and miserable ... It's not a good place – shan't stay long – I'm better in a house – I'm miserable.*

He seemed not to know how close death was. A week later he moved from the sanatorium into a house to be cared for by Frieda and her daughter Barbara. The next day, 1 March 1930, he died. He was buried in Vence but five years later his remains were disinterred and cremated; his ashes were taken to Taos and placed in a little chapel, specially built for them on Kiowa Ranch where he had lived with Frieda.

In his novels Lawrence constantly drew upon his own life and background, frequently putting friends and acquaintances into his work

*The Collected Letters of D. H. Lawrence, p. 1245

and relating actual happenings scarcely disguised. The village of Eastwood, where he was born, provided the backcloth for *Sons and Lovers* and the characters and plot of that novel were taken directly from Lawrence's life until the death of his mother.

The Rainbow is not so frankly autobiographical, but does take its setting from the countryside familiar to Lawrence as a boy. Though he was born in a mining village, it was small and compact, with a population of no more than three and a half thousand. A stone's throw away from the ugly little house of his first memories the countryside began. Describing this home he wrote in his essay, 'Nottingham and the Mining Country':

> A field path came down under a great hawthorn hedge. On the other side was the brook, with the old sheep-bridge going over into the meadows. The hawthorn hedge by the brook had grown tall as tall trees, and we used to bathe from there in the dipping-hole, where the sheep were dipped . . . life was a curious cross between industrialism and the old agricultural England.*

It is this 'curious cross' which serves as the setting for *The Rainbow*. Marsh Farm, like the Chambers' farm, The Haggs, remained isolated, yet colliery machinery could be seen in the distance and the sound of the winding engines could be heard. On their visits to town the farmer and his labourers brushed shoulders with the men from the pits and town and country were frequently united by marriage.

The novel spans roughly the last sixty years of the nineteenth century, yet few of the momentous changes which took place during that time are mirrored in the novel, though the encroachment of industrial life upon the country is integral. Lawrence's concern is not with history in its wider sense, with its political, economic and social impact upon the world at large, but with a microcosm, or little world, centred on the Brangwen's Farm in the Erewash Valley on the border between Derbyshire and Nottinghamshire. He traces the growth in awareness of the Brangwen family from the undeveloped sensitivity of young Tom in the 1860s to the intense, vital hopes of Ursula at the turn of the century. The great liberating movements of the nineteenth century throughout Europe and America are compressed into the yearning and aspiration of the Brangwen family to move out of its own little world into a freedom of the spirit, symbolised for Tom by Lydia Lensky, for William by Anna and, finally, for Ursula, not by a union with Skrebensky but by her rejection of him, by her new-found individuality and independence which was able to reject the romance of his foreignness and embrace the reality of her own future.

*Included in D. H. Lawrence, *Selected Essays*, Penguin Books, Harmondsworth, 1950, p. 117.

The main difficulties in the language of *The Rainbow* lie not so much in the use of dialect, though there are many dialect words, but in the somewhat turgid expression of the philosophic thought. To understand the events of the book on a simple level is generally no problem, but to appreciate the full significance of these events and their influence upon the inner lives of the protagonists requires careful, considered and repeated readings of the text. In Part 2 words which can be looked up in a good short dictionary, such as *The Concise Oxford Dictionary*, have not been explained, but any difficulties which might not easily be resolved by recourse to a dictionary are annotated. Further discussion of the text may be found in Parts 3 and 4.

A note on the text

The Rainbow was begun in 1913 and during the next two years Lawrence worked at trying to complete it. He found the material for the novel difficult to contain and in January 1915 he decided to make two novels out of the manuscript which he had originally called *The Sisters*. Much of the material was put aside and eventually became *Women in Love* (1920). The first part was developed and *The Rainbow* was published by Methuen on 30 September 1915. In November 1915 it was suppressed under the Obscene Publications Act and the edition was destroyed.

It was not republished in Britain until 1926 when Martin Secker published a slightly revised version, which was reprinted a number of times.

The original text of 1915 was republished by Penguin Books in 1949, in association with William Heinemann Limited.

The first Phoenix Edition was published in 1955 by Heinemann and republished a number of times up to 1968.

The Phoenix Edition published in 1971 restored the original text of 1915. This is now considered to be the definitive text of *The Rainbow*.

Part 2

Summaries
of THE RAINBOW

A general summary

Marsh Farm has been the home of the Brangwens for generations; the men have tilled the soil and established their own roots deep in the heart of the country, whilst the women have dreamed dreams and yearned for something outside themselves and beyond even their own comprehension.

In the mid-nineteenth century Tom Brangwen, who has taken over the farm on his father's death, finds himself heir not only to the earthy solidity of the Brangwen men, but also to the outward yearning of the Brangwen women. He marries Lydia Lensky, the widow of a Polish doctor; she is six years older than he and the mother of a four-year-old child, Anna, but, for Tom, Lydia represents all the mystery, strangeness and otherness that his heart longs for. Their marriage is not an easy one. Lydia often lives in her old memories and Tom is frustrated, feeling himself unable to communicate with her. Soon after their marriage Lydia becomes pregnant and Tom, feeling that she has removed herself from him, turns to Anna; despite the subsequent birth of his own sons his affection for Anna remains the most constant relationship in his life.

Anna is bright and intelligent; she is sent first to the local school in Cossethay and then to a school for young ladies in Nottingham, but she is not interested in education. When she is eighteen Tom's nephew Will comes to stay in nearby Ilkeston whilst he is apprenticed as a draughtsman in a lace factory. She mocks him and admires him, and finally falls in love with him. Despite the opposition of her step-father Anna agrees to marry Will and the wedding is arranged with a big family gathering. Once he has accepted her loss, Tom Brangwen acts as a kindly and loving father, taking a cottage at Cossethay for the young couple and buying for Anna all sorts of things to make her household work easier.

The first days of the marriage are filled with a passionate obsession which is followed by a revulsion, an unease. Anna grows to hate Will's interest and absorption in the church and in church art and despises his hobby of wood-carving; in his turn, he rages when she takes out her sewing-machine in the evening and pretends to have forgotten that it is time to make his tea. Their marriage alternates between periods of exaltation and of misery, until the birth of their first child, Ursula, gives

Anna a fulfilment which Will alone is unable to give her. About this time Anna renews her acquaintance with one of her countrymen, Baron Skrebensky, and meets his small son who is later to play a part in the Brangwen history.

As Tom with Anna, so Will finds himself passionately absorbed in his daughter's life. With the birth of their second child, Gudrun, Will takes Ursula for his own and a warm, almost obsessive relationship grows up between them.

When Ursula is eight years old Tom Brangwen is drowned in an accident and Lydia is left a widow, living on at Marsh Farm with her sons Tom and Fred. Ursula becomes a frequent visitor to her grandmother and Lydia tells the child of her Polish ancestry and of her true grandfather, Paul Lensky.

Ursula and her sisters now attend the little church school in Cossethay and mix with the other village children, befriending and quarrelling with them by turns. At last, when she is twelve years old, she is sent to school in Nottingham and is able to begin to wean herself from the sprawling domesticity of her home life and the responsibilities of the brood of younger children. Gudrun soon joins her at school, but whilst Ursula is quick and bright, Gudrun is unwilling to accept learning and does not enjoy school; nevertheless, the two sisters cling to each other.

As Ursula slowly matures she passes through a period of adolescent turmoil, bewilderment with her family, a bout of religion and then a romantic love affair with the young Skrebensky, the son of her grandmother's friend. Now a junior officer in the British Army, Anton Skrebensky visits Marsh Farm with Ursula's uncle, Tom; on his second visit there he and Ursula become lovers. When he leaves to go to the Boer War, Ursula is distraught. She continues with her studies in a mechanical fashion until she is caught up in a brief lesbian affair with one of her teachers, Winifred Inger. She finishes her studies and leaves school, still in a whirl of emotional instability but, preparing to cast off Miss Inger, she introduces her to her uncle Tom and the two decide to marry. Free of entanglements Ursula returns home to find her mother pregnant again. The disorder of the house and the wildness of the children cause tension between Ursula and Anna and she determines to leave home and earn her living as a teacher. When the possibility of a post in Kingston upon Thames offers itself to her, her father refuses to let her go. Instead he arranges for her to take a post in a school in the poor quarter of nearby Ilkeston. Though her soul rebels against it, Ursula accepts in order to give herself some measure of freedom. The school, however, is uncongenial, most of the teachers unfriendly, the headmaster a bully and her class undisciplined. Though she had wanted to give them love, hostility grows up between the children and Ursula and at last a crisis occurs in the classroom, in which she finds herself compelled to thrash a boy if she is to maintain any position of respect. Gradually she gains control but at a price she is hardly willing to pay. She now has the class under her control and her teaching becomes almost mechanical; she pins all her hopes on further study and the chance of reading for a degree.

During this time she has become friendly with Maggie Schofield, one of the other teachers at the school, and, visiting Maggie, she finds herself treated royally by her friend's brothers. The oldest, Anthony, falls in love with her and proposes marriage, but she rejects him, recognising his physical attraction, but knowing that they have no spiritual meeting-point. Now her time at the school is nearly at an end and this coincides with her father's appointment as Art and Handwork Instructor for the County of Nottingham; the family leave the cottage in Cossethay for a large modern house ien the colliery-town of Beldover.

The following October Ursula enters the University of Nottingham to read for her BA degree but gradually the life goes out of her studies and they seem to lack meaning for her. Then, suddenly, she hears from Anton Skrebensky again and resumes her affair with him, abandoning everything to the passion of the moment. He is due to go to India and proposes marriage but she at first refuses, not wishing the finality of linking her fate with his. She finishes her course at the university and fails her BA examinations, but the affair with Anton drags on and she drifts into a marriage agreement. Once the wedding arrangements are made, however, Ursula knows she cannot go on and breaks away from Anton; he, determined to take a wife to India with him, immediately proposes to his colonel's daughter and is accepted.

Meanwhile, Ursula has returned home to discover that she is expecting Skrebensky's child. Unaware of his marriage, she writes to him, telling him of the child and submitting herself to him. Then, her own decision made, she awaits his answer. Feeling cut off from her family she wanders about the countryside alone until a terrifying experience with a group of horses during a drenching rainstorm contributes to a breakdown. In the period of fever and delirium that follows she loses the child. Now the cable from Skrebensky which announces his marriage only serves to distress and anger her. She goes through a period of spiritual misery, fearing that she may never awaken from it until the vision of a rainbow, promise of hope to the world, brings her a mystic understanding and a new belief in the future.

Detailed summaries

Chapter I. How Tom Brangwen Married a Polish Lady: I

The novel opens with a general survey of the Brangwen family. Of farming stock, they have lived for generations at Marsh Farm, near the village of Cossethay on the border between Derbyshire and Nottinghamshire, beside the slow-running Erewash river. Two miles away, the church-tower of neighbouring Ilkeston dominates the landscape. Whilst not wealthy, the Brangwens have enough to make them independent. They cultivate the rich farmlands and the menfolk are identified with the natural power and creativity around them; content with their lot, they live fully in the activities which wrest their livelihood from the earth. The Brangwen women, on the other hand, look outward from their own narrow lives, seeing in the local clergymen and the gentlefolk at Shelly Hall the fuller life that education and experience bring. Less satisfied than their men, they aspire to something above and beyond them and in yearning towards these aspirations, they become more satisfied.

NOTES AND GLOSSARY:

Odyssey ... Penelope ... Ulysses ... Circe: Ulysses is the main protagonist of Homer's *Odyssey* and Penelope is his wife. In his wanderings Ulysses has many adventures, in one of which his followers are ensnared by the enchantress Circe, and turned into swine. Fortified by a magic potion, Ulysses forces Circe to release his followers; he then stays with her for a year and becomes the father of her son, Telegonus

leading shoot: the principal growing shoot of a plant

How Tom Brangwen Married a Polish Lady: II

During the 1840s the Industrial Revolution begins to impinge upon the life of the Brangwens. Collieries spring up around them and a canal is constructed across their fields; the railway runs along the valley bringing the possibility of easier communication between industrial and rural life. Marsh Farm remains remote, yet no longer isolated from the bustling life of the industrial townships around it. The Brangwen of this period has six children and it is with the life of Tom, the youngest, that the story is concerned. His mother's favourite, he is sent to the local Grammar School, but learning is a burden to him; when Tom is seventeen his father dies after an accident and the youth is left to run the farm. Six years later his mother dies and when his sister Effie gets married he is alone at Marsh Farm except for the serving-woman. He has a strange unsatisfied streak within him which neither drunkenness nor whoring can satisfy and after a brief indulgence in these follies he settles into a steady routine, but still yearns for something beyond. When a Polish woman, Lydia Lensky, widow of a doctor, comes to Cossethay as housekeeper to the vicar, Tom realises that she, with her foreign ways and remoteness from the everyday life of the village, has a strong attraction for him. She is older than Tom and has a four-year-old daughter, Anna; slowly and painfully, Tom tries to get to know Lydia, but he always feels rebuffed by her air of separateness. After a number of meetings at which both Tom and Lydia feel some magnetic attraction between them, but in which no word of love is spoken, Tom decides that he must marry her. On a cold March evening, dressed in his best clothes and with a bunch of daffodils in his hand, he goes up to the vicarage to propose. After a brief hesitation, Lydia accepts and their agreement to marry is followed by an ecstatic and wordless embrace before Tom leaves for Marsh Farm again.

This first chapter sets the scene for the novel both geographically and chronologically and introduces the reader to the Brangwen family. It also prepares the ground for the method of the novel – the exposure of the usually hidden part of character; Tom Brangwen is seen not only as a small farmer, but also as a man with aspirations beyond himself, a man whose yearnings to fulfil himself influence his whole character and way of life. His inner soul is exposed through the use of rich symbolism, expressed principally through cosmic imagery, through the images of birth, creativity and the natural cycle and through animals.

NOTES AND GLOSSARY:

pedgill: *(dialect)* pronounced 'peggle'; to struggle or labour

silk purse . . . sow's ear: an old proverb

David and Jonathan: a reference to the biblical friendship of David and Jonathan, the son of King Saul. See 1 Samuel 18:1–4

mardy: *(dialect)* spoilt

Prometheus Bound: in Greek mythology Prometheus was a demigod who defied Zeus by giving fire to Man. Zeus punished him by chaining him to a rock on Mount Caucasus where, during the day, an eagle pecked his liver and, at night, his liver was restored again in order for him to suffer the next day. Aeschylus (525–456BC) based his play, *Prometheus Bound*, on this story

What the Hanover?: *(dialect)* a mild oath

britching: *(dialect)* pulling back

sluther up: *(dialect)* hurry up

clutterin' at the nipple: he means that she is not a baby

Chapter II. They Live at the Marsh

The daughter of an aristocratic Polish landowner, Lydia had married a young doctor, Paul Lensky, an active patriot and revolutionary. They had two children, both of whom died from diphtheria before their parents were forced to flee to London as refugees. There, Lensky worked tirelessly for his cause, but soon after his third child, Anna, was born, he died, leaving Lydia unprovided for in a foreign land. She went to Yorkshire as nurse to an aged rector; on his death she went to Cossethay and her fortune became linked with that of Tom Brangwen.

Like Tom, Lydia too feels a strange attraction between them, yet when she has accepted him and is ready to offer herself wholly to him, he is bound by inhibitions which stifle her soul. The wedding takes place and Lydia moves with Anna to Marsh Farm. The relationship between Tom and Lydia is a difficult one, for it is only rarely that they are fully attuned to each other. When Lydia becomes pregnant Tom finds himself thrown more and more into the company of the child Anna; the night his first son is born Tom helps Anna through a storm of tears and passion to peaceful sleep and the two gradually become devoted to each other.

After the introductory section the events of the first chapter were seen mainly through the eyes of Tom Brangwen. This second chapter shifts the perspective in order to look at Lydia's earlier life until her marriage to Tom. After this, the consciousness of Tom takes over again and though Lydia's inner feelings are described it is generally through the eyes of her husband. The dominance of Anna in this chapter prepares us for her story to follow that of Tom.

NOTES AND GLOSSARY:

trial ... Gethsemane ... Triumphal Entry: a reference to the story of Jesus in the Bible, to his trial before Pilate, his agony in the Garden of Gethsemane and his triumphal entry into Jerusalem seated on an ass's colt. See, for these stories, St Luke 23:1–26, 22:39–53 and 19:28–40 respectively

supper-up: *(dialect)* give the last food of the day to

Chapter III. Childhood of Anna Lensky

When Tom's son is born Tom himself feels that he is cut off from his wife as she is absorbed in the baby. He and Anna enjoy each other's companionship more and more; they play together and he teaches her nursery rhymes. She goes everywhere with him, round the farm, driving in the little horse-carriage to the town and finally every week to the market. Tom's friends by turns tease her and spoil her and he himself is very proud of her and wants to make her into a lady.

Tom's elder brother Alfred is illicitly connected with a genteel widow living in the village of Wirksworth and Tom, out of curiosity, goes to visit her one day. He is profoundly impressed by the gentility and superiority of the woman and by the cultured air of her drawing-room with its many books and its piano. Once again he yearns for something beyond the limitations of his own life and at home Lydia recognises his dissatisfaction. When she reproaches him with it he is at first astonished, but this episode ends in a tender reconciliation in which new and deep understanding of each other comes to the couple. This peace and joy between them releases Anna from the tensions of having to resolve the troubles between the two and she is able to enjoy her childhood.

Despite the title of this chapter it is only partially concerned with Anna, for Lawrence is attempting to chart the progress in the relationship between Lydia and Tom. The scenes with Anna serve a dual purpose for they serve to prepare us for our later interest in Anna's character, but at the same time they show us another side of Tom – gay, cheerful, devoted and free of the complications which bedevil his marital relationship.

NOTES AND GLOSSARY:

the blackbirds' singing: they are quoting from the nursery rhyme: Sing a song of sixpence/A pocketful of rye,/Four and twenty blackbirds/Baked in a pie;/When the pie was opened/The birds began to sing;/Now wasn't it a dainty dish/To set before the king?

Pocketful of posies: Anna has confused 'Sing a song of sixpence' with: Ring a ring a roses, A pocketful of posies, Atchoo! Atchoo! We all fall down

fawce: *(dialect)* precocious

sharp-shins: *(dialect)* clever child

Wheriver dun they . . .?: *(dialect)* 'Where do they . . .?'

wambling: *(dialect)* walking unsteadily

Herbert Spencer: Spencer (1820–1903) was an English philosopher

Browning: the Victorian poet, Robert Browning (1812–89)

pillar of fire . . . of cloud: when the Israelites fled from Egypt, God went before them in a pillar of cloud by day and in a pillar of fire by night (Exodus 13:21–2)

Chapter IV. Girlhood of Anna Brangwen

At the age of nine Anna is sent to school, first to the village school in Cossethay and later to a school for young ladies in Nottingham. At neither school does she make any real friends and she comes to the conclusion that education is pointless and her teachers coarse-souled. The first person outside her own family group to make any real impression on her is an old Polish friend of her mother, Baron Skrebensky, now vicar of a country parish in Yorkshire. She admires most his aristocratic bearing and freedom of spirit because they chime with her desire to be a lady. Tom encourages Anna and is delighted with her pride, though sad when at times she seems to despise him.

During her adolescent years Anna goes through the turmoil of religious doubt and general uncertainty about life, not knowing what she wants, emotional and withdrawn by turns. Then, when she is eighteen, her cousin Will Brangwen, son of Tom's brother Alfred, comes to work as junior draughtsman in a lace factory in Ilkeston. When he is invited to Marsh Farm, Anna is strangely excited at his arrival and disgraces herself at church by laughing uncontrolledly at his singing. Gradually the two fall in love with each other, though at first neither knows how to express it. Will's hobby is wood-carving and he makes Anna a present of a butter-stamper, which she uses on the butter at the farm. Soon after, he begins a carving depicting the Creation of Eve for a church panel, inspired to carve the Eve by his love for Anna. A strange night-harvesting episode, in which Will and Anna set up the sheaves in shocks, results in their deciding to get married.

At first Tom Brangwen is angry, because he realises that he must lose Anna, that life is slipping through his fingers and that he is being superseded by youth. Once he has accepted this, however, he sets out to please Anna by helping her financially. He takes a lease on a cottage in Cossethay for the young couple, hands over to Will shares for £2500 which he had put aside for Anna, and week by week enjoys bringing little household gadgets, such as a meat-mincer, an egg-whisk or a mangle home for her.

Lawrence is concerned with several generations of the Brangwen family and here, through the replacement in Anna's affections of Tom by Will, he is showing the inevitable cycle of history in which the older generation is unwillingly compelled to give way to the younger. By the end of this chapter the main focus of interest has shifted from Tom and Lydia to Anna and Will.

NOTES AND GLOSSARY:

Mr Gladstone: William Ewart Gladstone (1809–98) was Prime Minister of Great Britain, 1868–74, 1880–5, 1886 and 1892–4

knight of Malta: a name at one time applied to the Knights Hospitallers who had their headquarters in Malta during the sixteenth century. The term Knight of Malta is now (and was when *The Rainbow* was written) extinct. The present-day descendant of the Knights Hospitallers is the St John Ambulance Association, founded in 1877

As You Like It: a play by William Shakespeare, 1599

Goose Fair: Goose Fairs were once held in many English towns at Michaelmas (29 September). The Nottingham Goose Fair (which is still held) was one of the most important

Ave Maria . . . mortis nostrae: (Latin) a prayer used in the telling of the rosary beads. It runs: 'Hail Mary, full of grace, the Lord is with thee, blessed art thou among women and blessed is Jesus, the fruit of thy womb. Holy Mary, Mother of God, pray for us sinners now and in the hour of our death'

snirt: *(dialect)* a noise made through the nose when attempting to suppress laughter

Ruskin: John Ruskin (1819–1900), an English essayist and art critic

Gothic . . . Renaissance . . . Norman: styles of church architecture

the Devil looking over Lincoln: this term is generally used of a backbiter or spiteful critic. Lawrence uses it as a physical image, but Tom's satisfaction with the thought is because of its meaning. The actual reference, according to *Brewer's Dictionary of Phrase and Fable*, is either to a stone picture which overlooked Lincoln College, Oxford, or to one of the grotesque sculptures at Lincoln Cathedral

Creation of Eve: the story of the creation of Eve from one of Adam's ribs is told in Genesis 2:21–5

dolly-tub: *(dialect)* a kind of wash-tub widely used before automatic machines were introduced

---

Chapter V. Wedding at the Marsh

The wedding day arrives at last and all the Brangwen family gathers for the celebration. Anna, beautiful and elegant, is escorted to the church by her father and, after the marriage service is over, the whole party goes first to Will and Anna's little cottage to drink to the newly married couple; then they go to Marsh Farm where the wedding meal has been prepared. Tom Brangwen tries to make a speech, but is constantly interrupted by his brothers and their wives. Since it is just before Christmas the company is entertained first by a band of carol singers and then by an old Christmas play. Finally, the evening draws to a close; the young couple return alone to their cottage and, once they have gone, Tom and some of the other men decide to go and sing carols outside their windows.

Here Tom's old uncertainties and longings are seen again as Anna's marriage recalls to him his own with Lydia. By the end of the chapter, however, the centre of interest has shifted completely. It is with Anna and Will that the power of youth, life and emotion now lies.

NOTES AND GLOSSARY:

guysers: a band of people who go from door to door to perform plays, generally at Hallowe'en or Christmastide (from 'disguise')

old Johnny Roger: a colloquial term used to describe the Devil

---

Chapter VI. Anna Victrix

During the honeymoon period Will and Anna are at first engrossed in each other, staying in bed half the day and taking little notice of the outside world. This period of ecstasy makes Will feel disturbed at the defiance of natural order, but he comes to accept it. Then Anna moves into the world again by giving a tea-party; this angers Will and a feeling of tension arises between the two. The perfect communion of the early days is followed by unrest and dissension in which the souls of the young couple rebel against each other; their love is often indistinguishable from hate and each lacerates the emotions of the other. Sunday is particular torture to Anna, for Will's love of the church and easy acceptance of biblical teaching deeply angers her and she tries to undermine his beliefs, attacking both the symbols of his religion and the words of the Bible. They constantly goad each other to fury and are subsequently reconciled, only to quarrel again.

Then Anna discovers she is pregnant. For four days she waits for a suitable moment to tell Will, but their hearts are set against each other. She visits Marsh Farm and tells her parents about both her pregnancy and her quarrels with her husband. Though Tom criticises her he feels hatred towards Will. After his work Will is called into Marsh Farm and as he and Anna walk home that evening she tells him about the expected child and for a while happiness is restored to them. Yet the struggle continues again, with love and hate alternating. There is a strange scene in which Anna tries to assert herself by dancing naked in her bedroom at a late stage in her pregnancy; this infuriates Will, but he is unable to stand up against her. With the birth of the baby, Ursula, both Anna and Will relax into a brief period of peace with each other again, but they both feel obscurely that, somehow, Anna has won.

Interest in this chapter is not so much on the characters of Will and Anna, but in the relationship between them. By shifting the viewpoint from one to the other Lawrence is attempting to analyse this relationship in a depth of detail that is completely original. The symbol of the rainbow used towards the end of the chapter is recalled at the end of the book.

NOTES AND GLOSSARY:

Anna Victrix: *(Latin)* Anna, the Conqueror. Perhaps after Rossetti's Sonnet XXXIII from *The House of Life*, 'Venus Victrix'

in full hands: *(dialect)* with plenty to do

Tablets of Stone: a reference to Moses casting down the tablets of stone on which God's commandments had been written when he discovered that the Israelites had been worshipping a golden calf. See the Bible, Exodus 32:15–19

the Lord in two burning bushes . . . consumed: Moses was called to God's service by the voice of God from a burning bush which was not consumed. (Exodus 3:1–12)

the water turned to wine at Cana: in his first miracle Jesus turned water into wine at a wedding feast in Cana. See the Bible, St John 2:1–11

packet o' butterscotch: he is sarcastically suggesting that she is always sweet to Will

'Magnificat': this is the song of praise to God from Mary after the Annunciation of the birth of Christ. See the Bible, St Luke 1:46–55

Fra Angelico: Giovanni da Fiesole (1387–1455), an Italian painter

David, who danced before the Lord: 'And David danced before the Lord with all his might.' See the Bible, 2 Samuel: 6.14

'Thou comest to me . . . into our hands': for the origin of these words see the Bible, 1 Samuel 17:45 and 46. The quotation is not quite accurate

Saul proclaiming his own kingship: Saul did not, in so many words, proclaim his kingship

ark . . . flood: a reference to the story of the flood and the ark which Noah built to preserve himself and his family. See the Bible, Genesis 7 and 8. This is an important reference because after the Flood was over God promised never again to flood the earth and the token of His covenant was the rainbow

Pisgah: this was the mountain which Moses ascended in order to view the Promised Land. See the Bible, Deuteronomy 3:27

the three witnesses . . . angel in the fire: a reference to the story of Shadrach, Meshach and Abednego who were cast bound into a burning fiery furnace by King Nebuchadnezzar. When the king looked into the furnace the three were alive and unbound and a fourth figure accompanied them. (Daniel 3:9–28)

Chapter VII. The Cathedral

This chapter begins with a flashback to a time before the birth of Ursula when Anna and Will go on a visit to Baron Skrebensky and his second wife. The older couple are both magnetic and elusive. Will finds, as his father-in-law found before him, that the Baroness teases and tempts him, openly flaunting her sexuality, but at the same time repulsing him, making clear her superiority. Anna is intrigued by the Baron who, though old and wizened, has a fiery quality inside him which attracts her. During this visit the Baron's infant son is introduced to the reader; later he is to figure largely in the life of Ursula.

From Baron Skrebensky's house Anna and Will make a visit to Lincoln Cathedral. The cathedral moves each of them in a different way. Will is moved by a deep spiritual reverence for the beauty, mystery and rich life of the building; Anna, on the other hand, is willing to be attracted only by the human quality of the stone carvings and reads her own drama into the little stone faces. With calculated meanness she takes away Will's joy in the perfection and wholeness of the cathedral itself.

At home she takes the same attitude to him and to the Church, mocking him when in speechless anger he kneels beside his bed to pray. Yet, with the birth of Ursula, a calmness gradually descends upon the household and Anna begins to have an understanding and respect for Will.

Here we see that Lawrence's concern in this novel is not with event, but with character. The visit to the Skrebenskys is uneventful but the four characters involved are illuminated for us. Particularly striking is the use of metaphors such as 'ferret', 'weasel', 'stoat' to suggest the predatory nature of the Baroness. Likewise the descriptions of Lincoln Cathedral lead us to differentiate between the dark, mystical character of Will and the earthy, human nature of Anna.

NOTES AND GLOSSARY:

transitation: an obsolete word meaning 'the passing to and fro'
God burned no more in that bush: see the fourth note following Chapter VI, p. 22
serpent in his Eden: A reference to the story of the Fall of Man in the Bible, Genesis 3. Eve was tempted by the serpent, representing Satan, to sin against God's commands; in her turn she tempted Adam

---

Chapter VIII. The Child

As Ursula grows, a strong bond develops between her and her father. When a second child, Gudrun, is born, Will devotes himself to the older girl and she goes everywhere with him. He makes baby-furniture for her and wooden dolls, helps to bath her and often takes her into the church whilst he practises the organ. Sometimes a spirit of evil moves him to test the child, and he subjects her, together with himself, to frightening physical experiences; at one time he jumps naked off the bridge into the canal with the naked Ursula clinging to his neck; another time he takes her to the fair and swings her up in the swing-boat until she is sick. The child often finds it difficult to understand his moods and resents his reproofs but she continues to love him most.

The years pass and two more girls are born to Anna. Now Will, like his father before him, begins to get restless. He goes out on his own, not caring for his family responsibilities. One Saturday night he goes to the Empire Theatre in Nottingham to see a variety show. Finding himself sitting next to two girls he decides to attract the pretty, common one. After the show he asks them both to coffee but the other girl refuses; so he takes the first girl to the tea-shop and then asks her for a walk; they go through the streets and turn into the park, where he tries, unsuccessfully, to seduce her. When he returns home Anna senses that something has happened, but she does not care and her very carelessness excites him to a passion of lust for her. For a while a new and entirely physical passion springs up between them. A fifth child, a boy, is born, and gradually Will grows into a responsible member of the community. He organises a woodwork class for the village boys and takes his place in the village life.

The close bond between Will and Ursula recalls that between Tom and Anna during Anna's childhood. There is a darkness in Will's character, however, that was never evident in that of Tom. Little Ursula is at the opposite pole, bringing light to set against his darkness.

NOTES AND GLOSSARY:

Twittermiss: a pet name, probably implying that the child is fidgety

sprit: *(dialect)* a sprout, or shoot

Education was in the forefront: the Education Act of 1870 introduced free compulsory Primary School education. This Act initiated an interest and progress in education during the following decades

---

Chapter IX. The Marsh and the Flood

Meanwhile Tom and Lydia continue to live at Marsh Farm with their sons, Tom and Fred. Tom the elder is short, dark, attractive, full of energy and intelligence. He is sent to London to study engineering and there he does well in his studies and prospers. Fred, on the other hand, is fair and blue-eyed, like the Brangwens. It is he who stays at home to help look after the farm. Though his father remains nominally in charge, Fred does most of the work.

One spring morning when Ursula is about eight years old, Tom drives to the Saturday market in Nottingham, telling his wife and son that he might be home late that night. By evening rain is falling heavily and Fred is restless and depressed; nevertheless, he and his mother and Tilly the serving-woman all finally go to bed and the farm is left in darkness.

Tom Brangwen, having spent the evening drinking at the Angel Inn in Nottingham, sets off for home in torrential rain; he is just sober enough to find his way to Cossethay and the farm, but there he finds several inches of water already cover the ground and the stable and outhouses are awash. Puzzled by the increasing volume of water he sets off to find where it is all coming from but, half-drunk, he stumbles and falls and, unable to rise, he is carried away by the flood of water; the banks of the canal have burst.

In the farm Lydia awakens and calls to Fred. They go downstairs and find the kitchen is deep in water. She senses that her husband is drowned and calls out to him. Fred goes to search but though he sees that the horse and trap are put away he cannot find his father. By morning the rain abates and Tom's dead body is discovered. It is carried to Anna's cottage and she and Will prepare the corpse for burial. After Tom's death Ursula becomes a regular visitor to her grandmother at Marsh Farm and Lydia tells her all about her Polish grandfather, Paul Lensky.

The first cycle of the Brangwens' history ends with Tom's death, but continuity is preserved through Ursula's visits to her grandmother and her dim understanding of her Polish heritage.

NOTES AND GLOSSARY:

slew: *(mining term)* a swamp or pool; generally used to describe the underground pools in a coal seam

Noah ... dove ... olive branch: in the biblical story of the flood Noah sent a dove from the ark window several times and when the flood abated it returned with an olive leaf in its beak. See the Bible, Genesis 8:8–11

falleth as rain on the just and unjust: '. . . he maketh his sun to rise on the evil and on the good, and sendeth rain on the just and on the unjust.' (St Matthew 5:45)

cut: *(dialect)* canal

'bobby-dazzlin': *(dialect)* strikingly beautiful

'In my father's house are many mansions': quoted from the Bible, St John 14:2

the beginning and the end: compare the words in the Bible from Revelation 1:8, 'I am Alpha and Omega, the beginning and the ending, saith the Lord'

Chapter X. The Widening Circle

Ursula, now growing up, finds herself increasingly in charge of the younger children and the representative of the Brangwen family. It is irksome to her that she is unable to have any privacy and that she is never considered as an individual. She often shuts herself away to read or think quietly; she lives in the world of her imagination, a part of the fairy-stories she had heard as a child; she is always disturbed, however, by her brother or sisters coming to find her.

When she is twelve, Ursula is sent to Nottingham Grammar School and for a while escapes the burden of home. Yet she still cherishes Sundays at home when the family goes to church together. Whilst preparations are made the whole house is in a turmoil, but churchgoing and the rest of the day which follows are times of peace. The idea of church and religion is challenging to Ursula. Like her father she has a mystical passion for the whole Christian story and ponders often on the words of the Bible.

Here Lawrence moves into the consciousness of Ursula and uses her as mouthpiece for the wonder and doubt of his own mysticism. The story stands still whilst Ursula explores her own mind. Though the ideas are very true to the thoughts of a serious adolescent girl, the self-absorption of this chapter verges on the tedious.

NOTES AND GLOSSARY:

dursn't: *(dialect)* dare not

Rubens: Peter Paul Rubens (1577–1640), a Flemish painter

Idylls of the King: by Alfred, Lord Tennyson (1809–1902). The lines quoted are the opening lines of 'Lancelot and Elaine': the third line is slightly misquoted

without spot or blemish: Compare the Bible, I Peter 1:19, '. . . the precious blood of Christ, as of a lamb without blemish and without spot'

J'ai donné . . . petit frère: *(French)* 'I gave the bread to my little brother'

sluthered: *(dialect)* falling in a slatternly fashion

Il était . . . patapon: a well-known French folk-song, 'There was a shepherd . . .'

a voice . . . calling 'Samuel, Samuel!': God called to Samuel in the night to tell him that his master Eli was to be punished for his wrongdoing; see the Bible, 1 Samuel 3

Sin, the serpent: see the third note following Chapter VII above, p. 23

Judas with the money and the kiss: Judas Iscariot, one of Christ's twelve disciples, betrayed Jesus for thirty pieces of silver; he indicated to the soldiers whom to seize by kissing Jesus; (St Matthew 26:47–50 and 27:3–10)

telling one to put one's finger into His wounds: after Christ's resurrection Thomas, one of the twelve disciples, was told that He had risen and he said, 'Except I shall see in his hands the print of the nails, and put my finger into the print of the nails, and thrust my hand into his side I will not believe'. Some days later Christ appeared before Thomas and told him to put his finger into His wounds; (St John 20:24–9)

fettling: *(dialect)* providing for

'The Sons of God ... men of renown': from the Bible, Genesis 6:2–4

Jove had become a bull ... hero: the title Jove is generally given to the Roman God Jupiter, though many of the stories about him belong to the Greek God Zeus; it was Zeus who, taking the form of a bull, seduced the Palestinian princess Europa and carried her off on his back to Crete

Pan: the Greek god of flocks and shepherds

Bacchus: the Greek and Roman god of wine

Apollo: a powerful Greek god, known variously as god of light, healing, music, poetry, prophecy and manly beauty

'It is easier ... enter into heaven': a not quite accurate quotation, the origin of which may be found in the Bible, in St Matthew 19:24, St Mark 10:25 or St Luke 18:25

Giotto: Giotto di Bondone (1266–1337), a Florentine painter renowned as the founder of modern painting

Fra Angelico: see eighth note following Chapter VI above, p 22

Filippo Lippi: (*c.* 1406–69), a Florentine painter

Raphael: Raphael Santi (1483–1520), an Italian painter of the Roman school

'Mary! ... ascended to my father': from the Bible, St John 20:16–17

Chapter XI. First Love

As she grows into adolescence, Ursula is less and less willing to accept the mystic spirituality of the biblical stories. With the realisation of her own selfhood she feels that her religion must be able to help her live her weekday life. So she rejects the idealism of Christianity and turns again to a life of the imagination, becoming in her dreams rich, great, or heroic by turns; yet she constantly yearns back to the time of her ecstatic acceptance of religious mysteries.

At this time, with her soul open for some new influence, Anton Skrebensky, son of her grandmother's old friend, the Baron, comes into her life. His parents are now dead and he has joined the army; he comes with Ursula's uncle Tom to stay at Marsh Farm. The two young people are attracted to each other and he becomes a constant visitor to the cottage. He takes her to neighbouring Derby and they visit the fair together; that evening they kiss for the first time. Then his leave ends and he returns to his army unit. They exchange a few post-cards and she makes a cake for his birthday. When her uncle Fred decides to marry a local schoolteacher great celebrations are planned and Skrebensky is invited to the wedding.

Between the marriage service and the wedding feast Anton and Ursula walk beside the canal and, seeing a family on a barge she asks if she can go aboard and look round. The bargeman invites her and she is delighted to see that his wife has a small baby. She asks if she can hold it and what its name is. The parents decide to call the baby Ursula after their visitor and Ursula is delighted. Skrebensky is annoyed at this escapade, but later that evening the two become lovers, or so it would seem. He finds the experience unsatisfying and feels that in some subtle way she is destroying him. He returns once more to his regiment; soon after, war is declared against the Boers. Anton is sent to South Africa but comes to the Marsh for a day before he leaves. Yet the two seem to have lost contact and they part without warmth at the station.

The focus of the story has now shifted completely to Ursula, yet there are constant reminders of the cycle of family history repeating itself: she and Anton walk under the ash-trees on Cossethay hill 'where her grandfather had walked with his daffodils to make his proposal, and where her mother had gone with her young husband.' Ursula shares her father's mystic beliefs and inherits her mother's doubts; though the book reflects change, it also maintains continuity, particularly in the symbol of the rainbow which, once of significance to Anna, is now a vital part of Ursula's thought.

NOTES AND GLOSSARY:

climbing the tree with the short-statured man: when Jesus was passing
through Jericho, Zacchaeus wanted to see him.
Because he was too short to see in the crowd he
climbed a tree; there Jesus saw him and called him
by name. See the Bible, St Luke 19:1–6

walking . . . on the sea like the disciple: Jesus walked on the sea to join his
disciples in a boat and when Peter asked him if he
too could walk on the water, Jesus said 'Come'; so
Peter walked on the sea toward Jesus but when he
saw the waves were rough he was afraid and
immediately began to sink. See the Bible, St
Matthew 14:25–31

breaking the bread ... **five thousand people:** after Jesus had been talking to a huge multitude of people He fed them all on five loaves and two fishes. See St Matthew 14:15–21

blinded by the face of the Lord: Saul (before he was converted and renamed Paul) was persecuting the followers of Christ when, on his way to Damascus, Jesus appeared to him in a great light. He fell to the earth and when he arose he was blind. See the Bible, The Acts of the Apostles 9:1–9

following the pillar of cloud: see the ninth note following Chapter III above, p. 18

watching the bush ... **not burn away:** see the fourth note following Chapter VI above, p. 22

'Sell all thou hast, and give to the poor': For the origin of this quotation see St Matthew 19:21 or St Luke 18:22

turn the other cheek: 'whosoever shall smite thee on thy right cheek, turn to him the other also' (St Matthew 5:39)

'Oh, Jerusalem ... **and ye would not:** for the origin of this quotation see St Matthew 23:37 or St Luke 13:34

he would lift up the lambs in his arms: when Jesus called the children to Him He 'took them up in His arms ... and blessed them' (St Mark 10:16)

'Come unto me ... **give you rest':** from St Matthew 11:28

Adam ... **driven** ... **out of his native place:** a reference to Adam being cast out of the Garden of Eden. See Genesis 3:23–4

Once three angels ... **his household enriched for ever:** the three angels who visited Abraham came to tell him that his wife Sarah should bear a son. See Genesis 18:1–10

perpetuum mobile: *(Latin)* perpetual motion; the idea of a machine which once started goes on for ever without an energy supply

Wuthering Heights: by Emile Brontë (1818–48)

carousal: Lawrence presumably means 'carrousel' which is the French word for 'merry-go-round' or 'roundabout'

laisser-aller: *(French)* to let people do as they wish

fag-end: *(slang)* the last (useless) bit; originally the unsmoked end of a cigarette

'And God blessed Noah ... **destroy all flesh':** this series of quotations is taken from Genesis 9

Shem, Ham and Japheth: Noah's sons

'The very hairs of your head are all numbered': quoted from St Matthew 10:30 or St Luke 12:7

war ... **Boers in South Africa:** the Boer War was fought 1899–1902

the highest good of the greatest number: this is the doctrine of
Utilitarianism which flourished in the late eight-
eenth and early nineteenth centuries

like the angel before Balaam: Balaam, a hireling prophet, was
commanded by King Balak of Moab to curse the
Israelites. When he was riding on his ass to do as he
had been commanded an angel stood before him
with a sword and turned him aside from his way. See
Genesis 22:30–5

Chapter XII. Shame

Ursula is now almost at the end of her school career and she works at her
studies unwillingly but firmly because she believes that through her
academic work she may achieve a measure of independence. It is at this
time that she finds herself falling in love with Winifred Inger, one of her
schoolmistresses. The two are mutually attracted and a brief lesbian
affair ensues.

When the school year has ended Winifred Inger goes to London and
Ursula is left moping at Cossethay, but uncertain of her own feelings.
Then an invitation arrives from her uncle Tom to visit him in Yorkshire
where he has become a colliery manager. Ursula begins to imagine
marriage between her uncle and Winifred, so she invites the teacher too.
At her uncle's house Ursula is shocked to look at the surrounding town
with its sordid grimy houses and men and women without hope. Her
emotional reaction to it all separates her from the older couple whose
matter-of-fact acceptance of the mining community repels her. Toward
the end of the visit Winifred Inger and Tom Brangwen get engaged and
Ursula is glad to feel free of them both.

Ursula's emotional immaturity is evident in this chapter, not only in
her affair with Winifred Inger, but also in her whole attitude to life, in
her worship of nature and in her hatred of the sordid mining town where
her uncle lives. Yet every experience helps towards her understanding of
herself and thus towards her ultimate maturity.

NOTES AND GLOSSARY:

Newnham: a women's college at Cambridge University

Diana: Roman goddess of the moon, of hunting, and of
chastity; of great physical beauty she remained a
'maiden-goddess'

Moloch: a heathen deity whose worship required terrible
sacrifices

Napoleonic stupidity: Napoleon Buonaparte (1769–1821) was Emperor
of France, 1804–1815. He is seen as the epitome of
the lust for power

the lamb might lie down with the lion: a confusion, in fact, of a biblical
text. See the Bible, Isaiah 11:6, 'The wolf also shall
dwell with the lamb, and the leopard shall lie down
with the kid; and the calf and the young lion and the
fatling together; and a little child shall lead them'

Zolaesque: Emile Zola (1840–1902) was a French novelist

vogue la galere: *(French)* Literally, 'loose the galley!' the phrase
means idiomatically 'come what may'

Chapter XIII. The Man's World

Her schooldays now over, Ursula lives at home and helps with the
household chores, but the disorder of the domestic life and the
unruliness of the younger children anger and distress her. She begins to
hate her mother and her mother's way of life and decides that she must
escape from her home. Meanwhile, Will Brangwen turns again to his
wood-carving, then to painting and to the making of jewellery, always
seeking a satisfaction that he is unable to find in his own work.

Ursula writes to the headmistress of her old school for advice and is
told that she is qualified to take a post as an uncertificated teacher and
that after a year or two of this she could then go to college and take a
degree. Thus, Ursula tells her parents that she wishes to go out to work
and, believing that they acquiesce in her plan, she answers a number of
advertisements for assistant teachers. However, when she receives a
reply from Kingston-on-Thames, her father refuses to allow her to go
there and gets her a place in one of the Ilkeston schools.

The first morning she arrives in the school she finds the staff
indifferent and the children hostile. As time goes on she struggles to keep
her class under control, but also to hold on to her ideals. The headmaster
is a cruel bully and seems to hate her as much as he hates the children. He
takes particular pleasure in drawing attention to her inadequacies as a
teacher by punishing her class. Ursula is almost defeated by the misery
of her life in the school, but at last, taking the advice of one of the older
teachers, she violently canes an insolent boy; from that moment she
begins to gain control, but only at the expense of her own beliefs in
freedom and love because she has to subjugate the children in order to
live with them.

She has one friend in the school, Maggie Schofield, a slightly older
teacher, who has learned to overcome the problems of teaching and has
achieved a measure of independence. Although Maggie leaves the
school at the end of the year and finds a post elsewhere, she and Ursula
remain friends.

This is a very bitter chapter in which Lawrence expresses all his own
grievances about teaching and about education. He appears to have

little faith in the possibility of liberalising education, which in those days was conducted in a rigid and cruel disciplinarian fashion. So Ursula is unable to succeed in her idealistic attitudes towards teaching, success coming to her only when she is prepared to bully and to dominate.

NOTES AND GLOSSARY:

Donatello: Donati di Betto Bardi (?1386–1466), an Italian sculptor

Della Robbia: Luca della Robbia (?1400–82); an Italian artist and terracotta designer

Benvenuto Cellini: Cellini (1500–71) was an Italian sculptor and artist in metal

Jack-gnat: *(dialect)* a slightly contemptuous term suggesting impatience

Queen Anne house: dating from the time of Queen Anne (1702–14)

'Sweet Thames, run softly till I end my song': from *Prothalamion* by Edmund Spenser (?1552–99), 1.54

C'est la mère Michel . . . le lui rendra: from a French folk song, 'It's mother Michael who has lost her cat, who shouts through the window so that someone should return it to her'

jelly-tray: a kind of apparatus for making copies

Greuze: Jean Baptiste Greuze (1725–1805), a French painter

Reynolds: Sir Joshua Reynolds (1723–92), a British painter

mizzling: *(slang)* going away

Shelley: Percy Bysshe Shelley (1792–1822), an English poet

She shall be sportive . . . mountain spring: from 'Three years she grew in sun and shower' by William Wordsworth (1770–1850)

Chapter XIV. The Widening Circle

During the school holiday Ursula enjoys visiting Maggie Schofield and her family. Maggie's brothers are very attentive to their visitor and make her feel like a grand lady. Maggie's eldest brother Anthony is a market-gardener and Ursula delights in being told about all the growing plants. She feels a strong sexuality in Anthony which creates a physical bond between them, so that when he suddenly proposes to her one day she almost accepts, but she knows that their souls can never be together, so she rejects him, though all her life she is to remember his proposal.

School starts again and now Ursula is in control; the weeks and months pass and she is to leave her teaching and go to college. Her move is to coincide with an uprooting of her whole family, for her father accepts a post as Art and Handwork Instructor for the County of

Nottingham and they plan to leave the cottage in Cossethay and move to a new red-brick house in Beldover. At the end of the school year the headmaster and teachers say goodbye to Ursula and give her two books as a leaving present. Then follows the move, the furniture being carried in carts to the new house. Ursula and her father work together to bring some order to the confusion and at last the family is settled in happily. There is a striking change in mood between this chapter and the last. Ursula now accepts the school regime and feels that she is achieving something and the prospect of her father's new job brings hope to the family so that everything is light and gay.

NOTES AND GLOSSARY:

Coleridge:	Samuel Taylor Coleridge (1772–1834), an English poet, critic and philosopher
Botticelli:	Sandro Botticelli (*c*.1445–1510), an Italian painter
Swinburne:	Algernon Charles Swinburne (1837–1909), an English poet and critic
Meredith:	George Meredith (1829–1909), an English poet and novelist
at sixes and sevens:	in confusion

Chapter XV. The Bitterness of Ecstasy

After she has helped to put the house straight, Ursula revises some of her studies in preparation for going to college. Gudrun also has left school and is attending the Art School in Nottingham, so when Ursula's term begins the two girls travel each day together.

During her first year's study Ursula is enchanted with her new world, with the college building, with the lectures she hears and with the professors themselves. She makes friends with a girl called Dorothy Russell and the two work together, particularly at their botany. At the end of the year Ursula passes her Intermediate Arts examination and is now qualified to go on and take her degree.

In the summer she goes with her family to Scarborough for a month and after that she goes to visit her uncle Tom and Winifred who now have a small baby; there she feels ill at ease and is relieved to go home. When she returns to college, however, her studies begin to pall. Latin, French, Anglo-Saxon, all seem to her pointless; simultaneously the college and the professors lose their glamour for her. She decides to take an honours degree in Botany which is the one study she continues to enjoy; she hopes to gain her degree and find a place as mistress in some Grammar School.

Without joy, she moves towards her goal until, unexpectedly, just before Easter in her last year of college she hears again from Anton

Skrebensky. He is on leave before going to India and proposes to come to Nottingham to visit her. She is delighted to meet him again and immediately feels a strong physical bond with him. Her studies become insignificant to her, and she lives in and through her sensual passion for Skrebensky. In the Easter vacation they go away together, pretending they are married, first to London and then to Paris. On their way back to England they visit Rouen and there the seeds of their separation are sown. Ursula returns to college, and, left alone in London, Skrebensky writes to her pressing her to marry him; after a while she acquiesces almost without realising it. They become engaged and the wedding is arranged. Yet they have little in common except their physical lust for each other; her ideas make him angry and afraid, and she feels shut in by him and wants freedom.

When the time for her examinations arrives she goes to London to take them; after her practical examination they go out to dinner at a hotel on the river near Richmond. There he tries to fix the time for their wedding, but she tells him that she does not wish to marry him. To her dismay, he bursts into tears and she has to comfort him; this results in the breach being patched up, but Ursula knows that he has nothing to offer her except physical passion.

She fails her degree, but this does not incline her more towards marriage, because the thought of Skrebensky and India begins to offend her soul. They are both invited to a large house party in Lincolnshire and there she tests him by trying to gain complete satisfaction from their intimacy. The result is that he is left completely drained and they feel dead towards each other. Soon after, she leaves, not intending to see him again. For a while he is frantic, suffering anguish and dread; then he decides that he must marry to save himself from the horror of the separation. He proposes to his colonel's daughter, is accepted, the marriage is quickly arranged and he goes out with his new wife to India.

Here the hollowness of Skrebensky is fully evident; not only is he unable to satisfy Ursula but also he is afraid of the emptiness of his own life; he makes a hasty and loveless marriage in order to save face and to fill the gap left by Ursula. Nevertheless, the intensity of Ursula's relationship with him is not easy to accept, since her soul is not in it. Disillusion seemed inevitable, but Ursula's character is not enhanced by what appears to be her selfish physical indulgence at Skrebensky's expense, for she knows all the time that a full love for, and therefore an ultimate union with Skrebensky is not possible.

NOTES AND GLOSSARY:

Racine: Jean Baptiste Racine (1639–99), a French tragic dramatist

Livy: Titus Livius (59BC–AD17), a Roman historian

Horace:	Quintus Horatius Flaccus (65–8BC), a Roman poet
Chaucer:	Geoffrey Chaucer (?1340–1400), an English poet
Beowulf:	an old English epic poem of the early eighth century
jewjaws:	Lawrence obviously means 'gewgaws' – worthless trifles; there seems to be no other instance of the word being spelled in this way
nodalised:	Lawrence seems to have confused this word with 'nodulated', that is, characterised by nodular growths
Invisible Man:	the story of *The Invisible Man* by H. G. Wells (1866–1946) was first published in 1897

beast in sheep's clothing: the idea for this image may be found in St Matthew 7:15, 'Beware of false prophets, which come to you in sheep's clothing, but inwardly they are ravening wolves'

museau:	*(French)* snout
a half-sovereign:	a small gold coin which was worth the equivalent of 50p

Chapter XVI. The Rainbow

After she leaves Skrebensky, Ursula returns home, drained and empty. Her family are angry when she tells them that she has broken her engagement, but nothing is able to rouse her. Then she realises that she is pregnant with Skrebensky's child; part of her responds joyfully to the knowledge. She writes to Skrebensky begging his forgiveness, telling him of her pregnancy and offering to go to India and marry him.

As the days drag on and Ursula receives no answer to her letter, a revulsion begins to set in and she is overcome by profound apathy. On an October afternoon of torrential rain she slips out of the house to walk in the country. She walks across the fields and into the woods getting wetter and wetter until she turns back to go homewards by the common. Deep inside her is an inexplicable seed of fear, but she presses on; then suddenly she is aware of a group of horses which appear to be waiting for her; they gather on a log bridge which she has to pass over and as she moves towards it they move onwards and await her again. Suddenly they gallop, making a wide circle round her; with them behind her the way seems to be clear; she goes on, making for a gate in the field, when again the horses gallop towards her, this time veering slightly to pass her on the path. They gather again and Ursula, by now terrified, plans to climb a tree and drop down on the other side of the hedge; this she does as the horses gallop towards her again.

Eventually she arrives home, wet through and utterly distraught. She goes to bed and develops a delirious illness which is some sort of nervous breakdown. During her illness she loses the child, but she had already decided not to unite her life with that of Skrebensky. When she receives a cable from him which tells her of his marriage it merely makes her despise him.

Convalescent, her mind strives to find a purpose in life, to seek 'the creation of the living God'. The mining community around her seems to be dead and life completely corrupt. Then she looks out of the window one day and sees a rainbow begin to form. She seizes for herself God's promise and at last hope returns to her and faith in the future.

This last chapter is heavy with symbolic meaning. Ursula has to go through the crisis of suffering and physical destruction before she can emerge into new life. Only when she has overcome the physical strength and sexuality represented by the horses is she able to find spiritual hope.

NOTES AND GLOSSARY:

thankfully, on my knees, taking what God had given: compare Shakespeare's *As You Like It* III. 5. 57: Down on your knees,/And thank heaven fasting, for a good man's love

butt houses: (?) houses at the ends of rows

Part 3

Commentary

The novel as family chronicle

Establishing the Brangwens

From the very first sentence of *The Rainbow* Lawrence makes it clear
that he is concerned in this novel with chronicling the history of a family:
'The Brangwens had lived for generations on the Marsh Farm'. The
prelude to the opening chapter establishes the close affinity of the family
with the rich lands which they cultivate. Their very name has its roots far
back in the Old English language which their forebears spoke, for
'Brangwen' comes from 'brun-wine', meaning 'bright friend'. The whole
pattern of history and the cycle of the seasons is presented in the rhythm
of life of the Brangwen family; they

> came and went . . . . They felt the rush of the sap in spring . . . . They
> knew the intercourse between heaven and earth . . . . They took the
> udder of the cows . . . . They mounted their horses . . . the men were
> impregnated with the day, cattle and earth and vegetation and the sky.

The sense of life evolving from simple and primitive self-sufficiency into
the interdependence of a community is brilliantly evoked in these
opening pages. The book begins with the Brangwens, the 'fresh, blond,
slow-speaking people' whose patrimony is constantly divided from
generation to generation between the children. Yet, whilst the Brangwen
men toil to preserve the continuity and blood-intimacy of the family, the
women look outward to the world beyond Marsh Farm, aspiring
towards the spiritual fulfilment and natural superiority with which
education and experience endows such men as the Cossethay vicar and
his curate, or the aristocratic Hardy family at Shelly Hall. So the
Brangwens are drawn out of their self-contained life at Marsh Farm and
into the community in time for the first major encroachment of
industrial life upon the surrounding countryside, the building of a canal
across the farm meadows in 1840. The undifferentiated figures of the
early Brangwens help to universalise the chronicle, for the novel is not
only a family history but is at the same time a saga of the English
Midlands. By following the fortunes of successive generations, it charts
the slow absorption of rural and agricultural life into the pattern of
industrial England.

Though the canal helps to isolate Marsh Farm by shutting it off from Ilkeston, it also introduces new possibilities of trade, new routes of communication; it is followed by the expansion of the collieries, the building of the Midland Railway and the gradual encroachment of the town. It is the end of an era; the Brangwens feel like 'strangers in their own place'; they are no longer merely farmers but must become 'almost tradesmen' as well, producing supplies for the nearby town; the peace of the countryside is disturbed by the rhythmic sound of the winding engines from the colliery and the whistle of the trains; where before the church-tower at Ilkeston stood up in the 'empty sky', now the machines of the colliery are clearly visible, beyond them the miners' houses in the valley and further still the 'dim smoking hill of the town'.

The detailed chronicle of the Brangwen family begins with the Alfred Brangwen of the 1840s. Married to a woman from Heanor, he has in him the seeds of the genial good humour as well as of the brooding intense anger of the later Brangwens. Not significant as an individual, he is the representative father-figure of the chronicled history. Father of Tom, grandfather of Will and great-grandfather of Ursula, he bequeaths to his descendants not only the rich earth of Marsh Farm to be tilled for their livelihood, but also the inheritance of a tight-knit family lore and, through his wife, the yearning aspirations which move the succeeding generations. As the genealogy of the Bible family begins with Adam, that of *The Rainbow* begins with Alfred Brangwen.

His six children, born into mid-century Victorian England, fulfil destinies typical of their class and age; the eldest son runs away to sea; the second, Alfred, Will's father, moves to the town and takes a job as a lace designer, forsaking his rural heritage for a genteel marriage with the daughter of a chemist; Frank, the third son, takes over the butcher's business connected with the farm, drinks and neglects his trade. Of the two girls, the elder marries a collier, whilst the younger remains at home until both her parents are dead before she too marries. The youngest son Tom, his mother's favourite, is educated at the Grammar School, developing in sensitivity but making little progress academically. When he is seventeen his father dies in an accident and Tom is left to carry on at Marsh Farm.

Tom and Lydia

With Tom the detailed story of the individual Brangwens begins. He is, in looks, a typical Brangwen man, fair-haired, blue-eyed and heavy-limbed. He represents the continuity and stability of the Brangwen family, rooted in the heart of the land which they have farmed for generations and which he himself now clings to. Yet he represents too the social flux of his time; he is restless, filled with yearnings that he does not understand and cannot realise: 'He wanted to go away – right away. He dreamed of foreign parts. But somehow he had no contact with them. And it was a very strong root which held him to the Marsh, to his own house and land'.

This outward yearning in Tom, previously described by Lawrence as being present only in the Brangwen women, marks a new phase in the progress of the family, for the limited, inward-looking life of Marsh Farm is opened to outside influences. The chance encounter at Matlock with a little, wizened, middle-aged foreigner gives Tom a sudden insight into an unknown world; this world of gentlemanly courtesy, elegant and gracious good manners which the foreigner opens up for him remains vividly in his imagination, making him unable to settle back into the dull routine of his own life. Thus he is first attracted towards Lydia because he sees her as the fulfilment of his aspirations. A stranger, self-contained, self-absorbed, she seems to offer him that other life that so far has eluded him. When their eyes meet as they pass each other on the Nottingham road, Tom feels such a deep affinity with her that he cannot 'bear to think of anything,' lest it break into his vision of the 'far world, the fragile reality' which she represents.

Several critics have asserted that *The Rainbow* is a novel about marriage and, in the context of a chronicle history, marriage and family life are essentially part of the story. But Lawrence's interest in relationships goes beyond what a mere chronicle would require. He is absorbed by the subtle interplay between fact and imagination that draws people together or allows them to drift apart. Tom's courtship of Lydia hardly happens on the level of ordinary human contact. His intimacy with her progresses indirectly, through a conversation with his own servant Tilly, through a brief encounter after church with little Anna, through the purchase of butter for the vicar. In his mind, however, he has moved slowly but surely towards the decision to marry her. The scene of the proposal is evocative: Tom, carefully dressed in clean shirt and best clothes, his fair beard combed and trimmed, contrasts with the greying twilight and the wild violence of the wind; he picks a bunch of yellow daffodils from the orchard and tries to shelter them as he makes his way to the vicarage. There, still other contrasts are emphasised; by the vicarage path the few daffodils are bent in the wind and the crocuses are lying shattered. The darkness where Tom stands is broken by a shaft of light from the kitchen window and, peering through, he sees the bright face and fair hair of Anna and the dark, brooding face of Lydia as she prepares the child for bed. The motif of light and dark, which is used constantly throughout the novel, is here employed with telling effect as Tom in his black clothes, the darkness behind him, enters into the light of the kitchen as into a new life. Indeed, after Lydia has accepted him and they embrace, he drops briefly into a symbolic sleep from which he awakes 'newly created, as after a gestation, a new birth'.

The marriage of Tom and Lydia is the most successful relationship which Lawrence presents in this novel. Unhampered at the outset by any possibility of parental pressures, it is at bottom firmly based on Lydia's material and Tom's spiritual needs: she was 'poor, quite alone, and had had a hard time in London', whilst he knew himself as 'incomplete and subject ... without her he was nothing'. For Lydia and Anna, after their years of uncertainty and insecurity, Tom provides a stable and comfortable home and love, whilst she gives to him a new understanding of the meaning of life. It is not always a perfect union; particularly in her pregnancies Lydia often seems withdrawn, separate, whilst Tom, on his side, is unable to abandon himself wholly to her; but there is no taunting or baiting as there is later between Will and Anna; each respects the independent life of the other, yet finds fulfilment of self through the relationship, which 'contained bonds and constraints and labours, and still was complete liberty' (Chapter III).

In the true tradition of the chronicle the reader's concern with Tom and Lydia as individuals soon begins to give way to an interest in the next generation. Tom's role as husband is superseded by his role as father as the story progresses and attention switches from Lydia to her daughter. The shift is a gradual one, for Anna's childhood is warmed and cherished by Tom's protective love, so that he clings to her as she gropes towards an emotional understanding with Will. But the old, old story is re-enacted: age must give way to youth. Tom finds himself unable to maintain his pride of place in Anna's affections:

> He was isolated from her. There was a generation between them, he was old, he had died out from hot life. A great deal of ash was in his fire, cold ash .... he blamed himself, he sneered at himself for this clinging to the young, wanting the young to belong to him.
> The child who clung to him wanted her child-husband.
>
> (Chapter IV)

Anna and Will

A curiously contrived continuity is preserved in the marriage of the second generation, for Tom, through whom the line of descent would appear to be mandatory, is not the physical progenitor of those who follow, though, we are told, he 'never loved his own son as he loved his step-child Anna' (Chapter III). Yet Anna who is, through Tom, an adopted Brangwen becomes a Brangwen again when she marries Will, Tom's nephew. Thus, the Brangwen line continues directly from the patriarchal Alfred, Tom's father, through the effete Alfred, Will's father, whilst the continuity of the foreign element, introduced into the Brangwen line by Lydia, is contained in the life of Anna. Nevertheless, through an odd reversal, it is Anna who is the Brangwen of Marsh Farm and Will who is the intruder from outside, bringing with him a strangeness and mystery that is centred in his own intense and self-possessed life. Just as Tom had been moved at his first sight of Lydia by her quality of self-absorption and apartness, so Anna is elated by the unknown quality within Will and feels enriched by it. Emerging from moody adolescence, she is ready for new experiences and with Will 'Something strange had entered into her world, something entirely strange and unlike what she knew' (Chapter IV).

Yet the seeds of their later dissension are sown, though neither realises it at the time, at their first encounter when Anna is reduced to hysterical giggling by Will's singing and responses in the church; Will's spiritual life is bound up in the church, his apprehension of beauty and of mystery comes to him through the church and as their relationship progresses it is this that Anna cannot endure, that Will has a life in which she has no part and which she is unable to understand.

Their courtship is passionate, but it never achieves the finely strung accord of that of Tom and Lydia. The moonlight stooking scene, which Laurence Lerner has called the 'greatest love-scene in English fiction'*, is indeed both beautiful and moving, but though it ends in Will's proposal it shows a couple who are out of step; they finally submit to the passion of the moment, but they meet on no other plane. Tom's harsh question, 'And what are you going to marry on – your pound a week?' jars upon the apparent harmony, yet underlines the truth that their thoughts have not travelled beyond the moment of passion.

Their love lacks spirituality and hence, after their marriage when physical desire is partly sated, they have no real point of meeting; they are unable to communicate about the things that matter to them. When Will tries to talk to Anna about his wood-carving he is lost for words: 'He could not tell her any more. Why could he not tell her any more? She felt a pang of disconsolate sadness' (Chapter VI). So later when Anna finds that she is pregnant she cannot tell her husband, but in her anguish blurts it out to her parents whose love for her is more 'careful' and less demanding. The problem which Anna and Will have to face and which finally defeats their love for each other is that of recognising not only their unity as a married couple but also the separateness of identity of the other; but neither is willing to give way; Will tries to assert his rights as 'master' and Anna too tries, though more subtly, to dominate him: 'Anna Victrix', she proudly declares after Ursula's birth (Chapter VI).

As Anna finds her own self-confidence and power over Will through

*Laurence Lerner, *The Truthtellers*, Chatto and Windus, London, 1967, p. 204

her motherhood, it is perhaps not surprising that she gradually lapses into a 'long trance of complacent child-bearing' (Chapter XIII). Will, on the other hand, continues to struggle against being dominated, against seeing his spirit as subservient. Like Tom he turns to his daughter for affection but, unlike Tom, he uses this affection for the realisation of his own power:

> She loved him that he compelled her with his strength and decision. He was all-powerful, the tower of strength which rose out of her sight (Chapter VIII).

Ursula is absorbed, obsessed by her father's will and he in turn constantly desires the sensation of mastery. It is not enough that she adores him, he must constantly test her, force her to submit to his will until at last, after the episode at the fair with the swingboats, her physical sickness develops into a sickness of heart and

> for the first time in her life a disillusion came over her, something cold and isolating . . . . Her soul was dead towards him. It made her sick (Chapter VIII).

Throughout Ursula's childhood Anna and Will move along their parallel but separate ways. Their marriage survives a brief attempt at unfaithfulness on Will's part, followed by a renewed flare-up of physical passion between the two and then a settling down into routine. In middle age Will turns to public affairs and finds a new purpose in life. The love between him and Ursula, damaged but not utterly destroyed earlier, moves towards an ultimate disillusion as the girl tries to realise her own potentialities and he frustrates her at every turn, until at last she too makes a life of her own, separate, inviolable from her father's pervading will.

Ursula

Ursula is the last of the Brangwens that Lawrence deals with and we enter much more fully into her life. The preceding generations have occupied our interest for considerably less than half the book; the remainder is given to Ursula. She is of Lawrence's own generation, growing up in his world, with many of his aspirations and much of his own sensitivity accorded to her.

Whilst we were aware of the childhood of Anna it was not until adolescence that she usurped the reader's attention, whereas Ursula becomes a focal point for us in infancy and some of the early scenes in her life are among the most beautifully handled and evocative in the book. She is a child who from the first shows the sturdy independence inherited from her Polish ancestry. Despite her affection for and closeness to her father she lives her own self-contained life; when she goes to his workshed to be near him, she plays 'intent and absorbed, among the shavings and the little nogs of wood', neither touching him, nor communicating with him and whilst he practises the organ in the church Ursula is 'like a kitten playing by herself in the darkness' (Chapter VIII).

It is not until the time of Tom Brangwen's death that Ursula becomes aware of her own family history. During a visit to her grandmother at Marsh Farm the little girl questions Lydia about her two wedding rings and learns of Paul Lensky, her Polish grandfather. The story fires the child's imagination:

> [her] heart beat fast as she listened to these things. She could not understand, but she seemed to feel far-off things. It gave her a deep, joyous thrill, to know she hailed from far off, from Poland, and that dark-bearded impressive man. Strange, her antecedents were, and she felt fate on either side of her terrible (Chapter IX).

Meanwhile, Ursula has her own Brangwen life to live as the oldest of a large and unruly family. In Cossethay and the village school she is constantly at odds with the local children, drawn into quarrels which are not her own and beginning to consider the problems of inequality of wealth, intelligence and sensibility. Only when she is sent to school in Nottingham does she feel able to break away from the burdensome and constricting life of her own home.

As Ursula emerges into adolescence it is clear that her relationships are to be more complex than those of the generations which preceded her. She is first attracted to the other sex by Anton Skrebensky, for he seems to represent to her the outside world, the 'world of passions and lawlessness' which the sheltered life of the girl makes doubly fascinating. Yet though Lawrence calls the chapter in which the two meet 'First Love' there is very little real love in their early relationship. Ursula is in love, not with Skrebensky, but with the part of herself that she sees in him; 'she was in love with a vision of herself,' Lawrence explains, 'she saw as it were a fine little reflection of herself in his eyes' (Chapter XI). Skrebensky, on his side, is inflamed to passion by the unthinking and ingenuous sexuality of the girl.

It is difficult to be sure when they become lovers. If it is not in the stackyard on the night of her uncle Fred's wedding, then that scene is almost incomprehensible, yet much later in the book, in the chapter before the last, we are told, 'He had not taken her yet'. The love scenes between Ursula and Anton are the least satisfactory episodes in the book; the turgid language fails to give any genuine insight into Ursula's character and Skrebensky is never more than a cipher. Had he been real for Ursula, he might have become real for the reader too, but if there is anything in him to understand, she doesn't understand it: 'It seems to me,' she remarks, 'as if you weren't anybody – as if there weren't anybody there, where you are. Are you anybody really? You seem like nothing to me' (Chapter XI). In comparison with the vitality of the bargeman and his family, Anton is empty, lifeless, and after the scene on the barge in which Ursula gives both her name and her necklace to the baby, she feels that he 'has created a deadness round her, a sterility, as if the world were ashes' (Chapter XI). The affair pushes on to its inevitable conclusion, the broken engagement, the aborted baby and Ursula's breakdown. There, as far as *The Rainbow* is concerned, the chronicle ends, with the last of the Brangwens looking towards a new life.

The relationship with Skrebensky is not, of course, the only love relationship which Ursula forms during the course of the book. Unlike that of her forebears, her story does not simply chronicle birth, marriage, procreation and death, but is richly endowed with her varied experience. So, during Skrebensky's absence, whilst he is serving in the Boer War, and whilst Ursula is still at school, she has a brief lesbian affair with one of her schoolmistresses, Winifred Inger. On Ursula's side it is an adolescent passion, beginning in idealistic physical adoration and passing away in spiritual shame. It concludes with the not entirely convincing marriage which Ursula contrives to arrange between her uncle Tom and Winifred. For Ursula it ends in emptiness, just as the affair with Skrebensky does later.

By the time the novel ends, Ursula has suffered the disillusion of various failed relationships and is ready to build her life anew on 'a living fabric of Truth' which the rainbow symbolises for her. It is left to *Women in Love*, the novel which follows, to show her in a more honest and more lasting relationship.

The Bible, the Church and *The Rainbow*

While the earth remaineth, seedtime and harvest, and cold and heat, and summer and winter, and day and night shall not cease . . . .

And God said This is the token of the covenant which I make between me and you and every living creature that is with you, for perpetual generations.

I do set my bow in the cloud, and it shall be for a token of a covenant between me and the earth.

(Genesis 8:22; 9:12–13)

When Lawrence chose to call his novel 'The Rainbow' he was endowing it with a rich train of associations, for the rainbow is an evocative image, exciting wonder, a sense of mystery and an apprehension of beauty. Legend has lent to it a mythical and magical significance with stories of the Land at the End of the Rainbow and tales of bags of gold buried where the rainbow touches the earth. Above all, however, it is the sign of God's promise to Man that life will continue, that 'seedtime and harvest . . . shall not cease'. It is a symbol of hope that there will be a future, however destructive the past may have been.

The biblical story of Noah and the Flood, which may be found in Genesis, Chapters 6 to 9, is concerned with sin, punishment and redemption. Its end establishes the third or Noahic Dispensation* in which God covenants with Man not to destroy him. It is a covenant of hope and promise and its sign is the rainbow; this sign Lawrence uses as his title and it is a dominant image, recurring throughout the book.

The novel begins with the Brangwen family, the tillers of the soil, and with the cycle of seedtime and harvest. The parallel with the biblical story is quietly asserted, so that when after the birth of his son, Tom feels at odds with his own life and experiences dissatisfaction in his marriage, the reconciliation and harmony which follow are offered to the reader in terms of the rainbow symbol, Tom and Lydia meeting 'to the span of the heavens' (Chapter III). It is significant that in this, the most stable love relationship in the novel, the two together create the rainbow arch; standing apart, each respecting the independent life of the other, the central point of their meeting is one of mutual interdependence. Under the safety and hope of their love, the child Anna is able to play in freedom and peace.

Years later, when she herself is about to become a mother, Anna's own marriage passes through a crisis of misery and discontent, but neither Will nor Anna is able to allow the other spiritual independence and the marriage becomes a terrible and bitter struggle for domination. Finally it is Will who has to submit; he sees his situation in terms of the biblical flood: 'She was the ark, and the rest of the world was flood' (Chapter VI). Only by subduing his own desires can he 'come into his own existence . . . [be] born for a second time, born at last unto himself, out of the vast body of humanity'. Meanwhile, Anna with the birth of her baby, feels herself triumphing over him, 'Anna Victrix'; it is an uneven partnership; she glimpses 'A faint, gleaming horizon, a long way off, and a rainbow like an archway', but she and Will can never attain the perfection of the rainbow themselves. Just as she used to play beneath the arch as a child, now she remains under it, reflecting but not aspiring to its promise.

The baby born to Anna at this time is Ursula; she is the fulfilment of God's promise, symbolised by the rainbow, that life will continue. Tom's death in the flood whilst she is a child and her parents' failure to realise their 'own maximum [selves]' (Chapter XI) leave Ursula to struggle towards redemption alone. She first involves herself in the story

*This term is used of the time following God's covenant with Noah.

of the Flood and the Rainbow when in church as an adolescent she considers the words of Genesis, Chapter 6* about the 'Sons of God' and the 'daughters of men' and clings 'to the secret hope, the aspiration' that she will eventually marry one of these 'Sons of God' (Chapter X). Thus, when she first sees Anton Skrebensky, she '[lays] hold of him at once for her dreams'; he is one of 'those Sons of God who saw the daughters of men, that they were fair' (Chapter XI). Ursula, however, has confused the dream with the reality and she must suffer for it. Skrebensky is not one of the 'Sons of God'; he is a very ordinary young man with a foreign name and an outward air of independence; but generation after generation of Brangwens have been beguiled by the self-possession of another human being: so Tom was first attracted to Lydia and Anna to Will; now Ursula responds to Skrebensky's self-containment and does not realise until too late that his sense of isolation cannot be probed because there is nothing behind it. He is a mere façade. The physical passion which is generated between them can lead to nothing beyond itself. Thus Anton, who appears at first to suffer more, picks himself up, marries and, we must assume, pushes the past behind him, whilst Ursula emerges from the affair completely drained. Only by spiritual renewal is it possible for her to find herself again. Her mind dwells on the drabness and corruption around her and her soul's sickness erupts into a physical nausea, when suddenly she is moved by the beauty of a gradually forming rainbow:

> in the blowing clouds she saw a band of faint iridescence ... it gleamed fiercely, and, her heart anguished with hope, she sought the shadow of iris where the bow should be .... The arc bended and strengthened itself till it arched indomitable ... its arch the top of heaven (Chapter XVI).

The rainbow that Ursula sees at this time is not only the rainbow of the Noahic Covenant. So much of the book is in the tone of The Revelation of St John the Divine, but the ending is truly apocalyptic. Ursula's rainbow may be compared with that in Revelation 10:1, 'And I saw another mighty angel come down from heaven, clothed with a cloud: and a rainbow was upon his head, and his face was as it were the sun, and his feet as pillows of fire.' This verse follows the vision of the first woe with its locusts like horses and the destruction of a third of mankind. The rainbow is a reminder of God's original promise to Noah. For Ursula, it opens her eyes to a renewal of beauty and of wonder, to a sense of power outside herself and to the hope for a future with which the novel ends.

For a novel which had so much trouble with the censors, *The Rainbow*

---

*It is in this chapter of Genesis that God first threatens the destruction of mankind by Flood.

is remarkably packed with biblical reference. Though references to the story of the Flood are the most common, Lawrence ranges over many books of the Bible and appears to be equally familiar with both the Old and the New Testaments. The Bible is certainly his principal source of reference and he uses it directly to enrich his story by simile and comparison and indirectly in many biblical words or turns of phrase. Ursula ponders over a number of biblical stories and the whole effect cannot fail to impress the reader with the religious quality of much that Lawrence has to say.

The Church too figures largely in the novel. The first paragraph places Ilkeston Church in a dominating position *vis-à-vis* the surrounding countryside and shows it as a landmark to succeeding generations of Brangwens. Nearer home in the village of Cossethay the little church with its 'mere dozen pews' (Chapter I) is a focal point for the life of the community. In mid-century Victorian England regular church-going was a way of life and Cossethay Church, which despite its small size could boast both a vicar and a curate, is the centre of both the gossip and the aspirations of the women from the surrounding countryside.

In different ways the church influences the lives of the various Brangwens whose stories are told in *The Rainbow*. For Tom, who only occasionally goes to the Sunday services, the indirect influence of the local church is profound, for it is when Lydia comes to live in Cossethay as housekeeper to the vicar that Tom meets her; it is after a visit to church with his sister Effie that he first speaks to little Anna and it is when Lydia comes to Marsh Farm to buy butter for the vicar that he first speaks to her. He has to visit Lydia at the vicarage when he decides to propose to her and it is to the vicar he goes to ask for her. Yet this influence is merely peripheral; Tom never becomes involved in the life of the church and though he later sends his children there on Sundays he himself stays at home (Chapter IV).

For Will Brangwen it is different. He loves the church with a passion – not the living spiritual mystery but the material fabric of the church buildings themselves, the architecture, the stonework, the carvings, the stained glass. He loves the outward shows of religion and, caring little for the essence of Christianity, he invests these outward shows with the mystic meanings they symbolise. His passion, however, is the cause of rift between him and Anna. She resents his absorption in the church, finding herself left unsatisfied by the service and the sermons. What Will accepts with simplicity, Anna ridicules and, jealous of the passion that moves him, she sets out to destroy it. Yet he resurrects his belief and goes on loving the church 'for what it [tries] to represent, rather than for that which it does represent' (Chapter VIII). There is an uneasy truce between them as their children grow up. Whilst Anna dedicates her time to the needs of her latest baby Will occupies himself in service to the church, caring for 'the stone and woodwork, mending the organ and restoring a piece of broken carving, repairing the church furniture' (Chapter VII).

With Cossethay Church playing such a central role in Will's life it inevitably also becomes central for his children. From infancy Ursula had played in the church when Will was busy working there, or practising the organ and as she grows up the Sunday world of church and church services stands apart in her mind from the life of the weekday world. It is preceded by the Saturday night bathing of all the children and then, on Sunday morning before church they are all dressed in their clean clothes. As she gets older Ursula begins dimly to understand the wrangle between her parents over Will's attitude to the church and, we are told, she 'was with her father . . . she set more and more against her mother's practical indifference' (Chapter XI). For a while she is obsessed by the teachings of the church and then she breaks free, rejecting the 'Sunday world' for the 'weekday world' of action. It is at this crucial point in her understanding that she first meets Anton Skrebensky.

Without at first realising it, Skrebensky subtly undermines Ursula's love of the church. On their visit to Derby together they go first to the fair and then into the church. As they drive afterwards Skrebensky, stirred by their experience in the church together, tells her the story of a man in his regiment who always made love to his girl friend in a corner of Rochester Cathedral. It is a daring story for a young soldier to tell to a sixteen-year-old girl and it is clear from the tone of his conversation that he is testing her. On another of his early visits Ursula takes him across to the little church of Cossethay; with the afternoon sun shining through the stained glass of the windows it is a beautiful and romantic setting. 'What a perfect place for a rendezvous', breathes Skrebensky. His words suggest to her a daring new experience to be gained from the church:

Here, here she would assert her indomitable gorgeous female self, here. Here she would open her female flower like a flame, in this dimness that was more passionate than light (Chapter XI).

The kiss which follows her decision is the beginning of disillusion for, whilst to Ursula it is the fulfilment of bliss, Skrebensky wants more than she understands or is able to give.

From this time the church ceases to figure as an influence in Ursula's life. The previously frequent references to Sunday and to church-going disappear from the book. At the end, when Ursula has her vision of the rainbow, she seems to have transcended the material manifestation of the church with its stone arches and coloured windows, for what she sees is the 'great architecture of light and colour and the space of heaven' (Chapter XVI).

The Rainbow and education

In this novel Lawrence is not much concerned with the burning issues of the times, though the chronology of the novel spans the greater part of the nineteenth century with its sweeping social and governmental reforms. One of the concerns of the nineteenth century, however, was education and almost from the outset Lawrence suggests that this is to be a prominent theme in the book.

When the early Brangwen women compare their lot with that of Mrs Hardy of Shelly Hall, or their menfolk with Lord William Bentley, or the local vicar, or even the poor curate, they conclude that something is missing from their lives:

> it was a question of knowledge . . . . It was not money, nor even class. It was education and experience (Chapter I).

Thus the determination arises to ensure that their children are educated so that they may take their place with those other 'superior' beings.

In the 1850s two of the Brangwen sons are sent to school; Alfred (Will's father) is sent to school in Ilkeston but profits little from his experience, making progress in nothing except drawing. Tom, 'his mother's favourite', is sent to the Grammar School in Derby where, like Alfred, he makes little progress in knowledge, though he develops in sensibility. Lawrence, however, shows us little of the educative processes in the schools at the time; he concentrates on the reactions of the two boys to being educated and if any criticism is intended it appears to be against the idea of subjecting boys such as Alfred and Tom to the rigours of school education.

Anna, too, is sent to school, first to the little local school in Cossethay and later to a school for young ladies in Nottingham. Again Lawrence has little to say about the school itself, though, almost incidentally, he shows us a rote-learning method and a disciplinary regime which Anna despises and rebels against (Chapter IV). Nevertheless, young Tom Brangwen's education fulfils the aspirations of his forebears: from the High School he goes to London to study and from time to time he returns to Marsh Farm, 'curiously attractive, well-dressed, reserved, having by nature a subtle, refined manner' (Chapter IX).

Up to this point in the novel the practicalities of education have received no more than the passing notice that any chronicle of several generations might give. With Ursula it is different. She and her sisters go first to the Cossethay church school but when she is twelve she is sent to the Grammar School in Nottingham. This is for Ursula the gateway to hope. First, it is an escape from her own cramped and restricted life; she rejoices to be able 'to burst the narrow boundary of Cossethay, where only limited people [live]' (Chapter X). Secondly, she loves reading, passionately enjoys poetry and believes that education will liberate her soul. She is intelligent and quick at learning and before leaving school she matriculates in English, French, Latin, mathematics and history (Chapter XII). It is only when she leaves school that she begins to realise that for all her prized education she is qualified for very little. At that time it was far from usual for girls of even moderately well-off families to work for their living. They were lucky if they received an adequate education, but in any case it opened few doors. Ursula, therefore, like other girls of her social class, is expected by her parents to stay at home and help with the growing family.

Lawrence makes this an emotional issue, focusing on the sense of isolation, of frustration and of caged spiritual energy in Ursula. Only by a series of bitter battles with her father, in which her illusions are crushed one by one, is she able to shake herself even slightly free from the family shackles which bind her. Her own initiative is defeated, her desire to leave home and start afresh thwarted and in desperation she accepts a job as an uncertificated teacher in a school in a poor quarter in Ilkeston.

Lawrence's account of Ursula's experiences in this school is very subjective and the whole episode is both distressing and unsatisfying. Ursula approaches her new job with high ideals and excited hopes:

> She dreamed how she would make the little, ugly children love her. She would be so *personal*. Teachers were always so hard and impersonal. There was no vivid relationship. She would make everything personal and vivid, she would give herself, she would give, give, give all her great stores of wealth to her children, she would make them *so* happy, and they would prefer her to any teacher on the face of the earth .... She would be the gleaming sun of the school, the children would blossom like little weeds, the teachers like tall, hard plants would burst into rare flower (Chapter XIII).

Her first day dawns with a sense of disillusion – the late September morning is wet and dark; the other passengers on the tram are 'unliving, spectral people'; when she reaches the school it appears to her 'silent, deserted, like an empty prison'. The arrival of the other teachers and the children does not give Ursula much confidence; she finds the teachers 'so cocksure and so bossy' and when she first meets her class they are 'jerking their shoulders, tossing their hair, nudging, writhing, staring, grinning, whispering and twisting'.

The picture which Lawrence gives of the school is a highly critical one; the regimentation, the disciplinarian methods, the brutal canings are offset by no positive aspect of education. Ursula is thrown into her first day of teaching with no training and with scant assistance either from the headmaster or from the other teachers. When she faces Standard Five for her first lesson she is completely unprepared; a seventeen-year-old girl scarcely out of school herself, she is given no encouragement and no direction. She appears to receive no timetable, no teaching materials and no syllabus of work.

The possibility of a happier approach to teaching is offered to the reader through Maggie Schofield. Maggie has made a partial escape from the trials of 'the big room' and has thus thrown off to some extent the bullying domination of Mr Harby, the headmaster. Standard Three, which Maggie teaches, has a classroom standing by itself with

> windows on two sides, looking on to the playground .... there were pots of chrysanthemums and coloured leaves and a big jar of berries; there were pretty little pictures on the wall ... giving an air of intimacy (Chapter XIII).

However, despite the cheerful aspect of Maggie's classroom, and despite Maggie's friendly and tolerant character, Lawrence extracts no positive lessons from the contrast between her classroom and the rest of the school and he suggests the uselessness of effort and enterprise when he makes Maggie tell Ursula,

> the children are simply awful. You've got to *make* them do everything. Everything, everything has got to come out of you. Whatever they learn, you've got to force it into them – and that's how it is (Chapter XIII).

Likewise, for all her idealism, Ursula can succeed only by dominating the children and intimidating them both physically and spiritually. It is a jaundiced view of education which reflects Lawrence's own experiences as a pupil-teacher in 1902 and which has lost in the telling none of the bitterness and hatred he then felt towards the school system and the children placed in his care. Though later when teaching at the Davidson Road School in Croydon, he found his situation more congenial, he nevertheless wrote to Blanche Jennings on 15 December 1908, 'Thank the Lord we break up on the 23rd at noon .... I have smitten the Philistine with the rod, and they are subdued'. He sees education as a battle between the weak and the slightly less weak and appears to believe that children must be subjugated before they can be educated.

Ursula's experiences as a pupil-teacher are a further stage in her spiritual disillusion and as such are vital to the understanding of her character. However, the whole episode suggests a failure in Lawrence's artistic vision; it is too long-drawn-out, it inclines to the tedious and it suffers more than other episodes from the somewhat repetitive style of the book as a whole. Chapter XIII which encompasses it is the longest chapter in the novel and the strongly autobiographical element in it suggests it as the most self-indulgent.

In contrast the years which Ursula spends at university are glossed over. She goes into this new educational experience with illusions similar to those which had briefly enchanted her before she started teaching:

> She wanted all the students to have a high pure spirit, she wanted them to say only the real, genuine things, she wanted their faces to be still and luminous as the nuns' and the monks' faces (Chapter XV).

A measure of disillusion faces her almost immediately for the cold hard fact is that 'the girls chattered and giggled and were nervous, they were dressed up and frizzed, the men looked mean and clownish'. For a while an excitement in the acquisition of knowledge holds her in its grip, but it does not last. Again she fails to fulfil herself spiritually and, with the re-appearance of Skrebensky she loses herself in a frenzy of passion, fails her degree examinations and ends up as she had begun three years before with her matriculation as her only qualification to enable her to take 'a position in the world' (Chapter XIII).

Disillusioned in her relationship with her father, with her uncle Tom, with Winifred Inger, disillusioned with church, religion and education, Ursula is left with her passion for Skrebensky, which results in her final disillusionment. It is only in the sequel to *The Rainbow*, *Women in Love*, that Ursula returns to education again.

The style of *The Rainbow*

The Rainbow is generally considered one of Lawrence's major achievements, but it is by no means a perfect novel. It caused Lawrence much labour and uncertainty in the writing of it and went through many transformations before its final form was arrived at. Lawrence was determined to write a novel very different from his previous one, *Sons and Lovers*, and in its early stages he commented in a letter to Edward Garnett on 30 December 1913 that it was 'written in another language almost'. It is, in fact, a curiously uneven novel, beautiful, evocative, poetic prose being interspersed with purple passages and often with tiresomely repetitive words and phrases.

What is perhaps most striking is the scope of the novel, for in chronicling the history of the Brangwens Lawrence achieves far more than the story of a single family. The early Brangwens in particular are seen as representative human beings, set within the seasonal cycle, tilling the earth and tending the cattle until the building of the canal in 1840 heralds the onset of industrialisation. As the novel progresses, however, it is Man set in his perspective in the cosmic order that is emphasised. Tom Brangwen looks up at the stars while he is about his regular farm business and understands that he is:

> only fragmentary, something incomplete and subject. There were the stars in the dark heaven travelling, the whole host passing by on some eternal voyage. So he sat small and submissive to the greater ordering (Chapter I).

So the cosmic imagery takes its place in the novel. Chapter I closes, not with Tom's proposal to Lydia, but with his walk home afterwards when the sky and the clouds are made radiant by the 'liquid-brilliant' moon scudding across the night. There are many night scenes in the novel, the most memorable probably being the moonlight stooking scene of Chapter IV which ends in Will's proposal to Anna. There the rhythmic order of the stooking is punctuated by Anna turning into the moonlight each time she has placed her sheaves and the light from the moon 'laying bare her bosom'. When Will finally overtakes her and claims his kiss, his heart is 'white as a star'. Again, in Chapter XV, when Ursula and Skrebensky spend a summer night on the downs, the scene expands in time and space into a mirroring of the dawning of mankind. It is a striking passage which must be quoted at length:

it was as if the stars were lying with her and entering the unfathomable darkness of her womb, fathoming her at last . . . . They stood together on a high place, an earthwork of the stone-age men, watching for the light . . . . And she and he darkly, on an outpost of the darkness, stood watching for the dawn.

The light grew stronger, gushing up against the dark sapphire of the transparent night. The light grew stronger, whiter, then over it hovered a flush of rose . . . .

The rose hovered and quivered, burned, fused to flame, to a transient red . . . . There was a quivering, a powerful terrifying swim of molten light. Then the molten source itself surged forth, revealing itself. The sun was in the sky, too powerful to look at.

The cosmic power of this scene, the ordering of dark and light carry the reader far beyond the affairs of Ursula and Skrebensky into the wonder and mystery of the universe. At the same time, the language foreshadows the defeat of Skrebensky for he is unnecessary, ineffectual.

The cosmic imagery is reinforced by the imagery of birth and creativity and of light and dark which occurs throughout the book. Reference has already been made above to the occurrence of both these kinds of imagery during the telling of the episode of Tom's proposal to Lydia. Physical birth itself plays a significant part in the novel, for birth is not only a renewal of life but is also the confirmation of union. Tom is 'glad that his wife was mother of his child' (Chapter III) and both Will and Anna claim Ursula, he in sober certainty, she in ecstasy. However, beyond actual physical birth, birth imagery is used again and again to suggest an entering into a new kind of life and the book ends with such an image: intertwined with the vivid emergence of the rainbow is the emergence of the butterfly from its chrysalis, of the new-born baby from the womb, of the new corn from the seed, a multiple image of hope and light after the darkness of Ursula's despair.

The principal characters are frequently aligned with light or dark. The fair-haired Tom Brangwen, whom Anna thinks of as 'so fresh and free and all daylight' (Chapter VI), unites himself with Lydia, the dark and mysterious woman from the outer world. Anna marries Will and we are told, 'she was the daytime, the daylight, he was the shadow' (Chapter VIII). So in these two marriages the union of opposites achieves a fulfilment, but for Ursula and Skrebensky there is no such fulness in union. He represents not only darkness, and that a darkness which desires to engulf Ursula's brightness, wishing to 'enclose her in a net of shadow, of darkness' (Chapter XI), but he is also surrounded by death; in describing him Lawrence frequently uses such words as 'inert', 'deadness', 'sterility'; Skrebensky has nothing to bring to a union with Ursula. Alone therefore, she has to harmonise the dark with 'her own bright ecstasy' (Chapter XI) before cleansing and regeneration may come to her; it is this which she achieves in the closing pages.

Other images, clearly allied to those discussed above, are of doors, gates and windows, opening into new life or throwing out light upon darkness and, of course, always the biblical imagery, particularly that of the Transfiguration because the novel is concerned with change, with casting off the old life and entering upon the new.

It is almost impossible to do justice to Lawrence's use of imagery in *The Rainbow* in a short and logical sequence for the images are so many and so various. The reader may like to follow up for himself such imagery as that of birds, animals, flowers, fruit, rivers and springs, water in general, fire and flame, glass and crystal, the images of chaos and disintegration. The interweaving of these many images makes the texture of the novel very dense and at times almost claustrophobic.

The novel has often been criticised for being repetitive and over-written and there are grounds for both these criticisms. In general, the language serves the purpose of enriching the story, giving insights into character that simple, non-symbolic language is unable to give, interlayering the plot with levels of understanding that transcend the chronicled history giving it a spiritual significance. Nevertheless, there are times when the language becomes tedious, when the high-flown style ceases to contribute new ideas but merely offers the old again in repetitious fashion. Most irritating is the use of 'catch-words' such as 'maximum': that Ursula wishes 'to know her own maximum self' (Chapter XI) is understandable but is there real meaning in 'Sunday remained the maximum day of the week' (Chapter X)? Yet this said, the novel with all its faults is better than an emasculated version lacking all its beauties.

Part 4

Hints for study

NOTHING CAN BE a substitute for a thorough and careful reading of *The Rainbow* itself. Once it has been read, the story taken in and a general impression has been received, read it again, giving special attention to particular aspects of the novel. On your second reading take notes and jot down quotations; make sure that your note or quotation is followed by a bracketed page number (or chapter number if you are not using your own book and may have to use a different edition on a subsequent reading). What kind of things will you be looking at as you study the novel closely? Perhaps you should consider at least some of the following: (1) characters, (2) relationships, (3) settings, (4) religion, (5) education, (6) art and architecture, (7) imagery, and (8) language. Try to think of other interesting or significant aspects of the novel which you could add to this list. (Part 3 of these notes may help you.)

Always remember to return to the text in order to support or illustrate points you are making. Critics may suggest ideas to you, but you should ensure that you accept these ideas only if your own knowledge of the novel confirms them. A critic can be wrong; or two critics may disagree; even if you believe a critic to be right, check that the text is able to support his argument. Try to find quotations other than those he has used which could have been used on his side; are there passages in the novel which appear to refute his arguments? When you were reading Part 3 of these notes did you agree with everything that was said? If so, did you try to think of other quotations that supported what was said? If you disagreed, are you able to illustrate your own beliefs with quotations from the text?

A good way of getting to know a novel well is by examining a particular major incident and seeing how it bears on theme, plot, character and other aspects of the book. In examining one incident you are forced to examine a number of other incidents as well. Let us take as our example the episode in Chapter IV of Will Brangwen's first visit to Marsh Farm. Straight away it underlines the chronicling function of *The Rainbow*, for not only are two generations of the Brangwen family brought together but the similarity of events and character from generation to generation is emphasised. Will is the son of one of Tom's older brothers, Alfred, who after a disappointing school career in which he excelled in nothing but drawing, went to Nottingham as a draughtsman in a lace factory (Chapter I). Will is following in his father's footsteps, though he is reversing the geographical move and coming from Nottingham to Ilkeston. The incident throws light on several of the major characters – Tom, kindly, generous, good-humoured, intensely fond of his step-daughter; Anna, at her first moment of sexual awareness, concerned with external impressions, embarrassed with an adolescent's embarrassment, amused with a child's sense of humour and unable to participate in the mystic reverence which Will holds for the church; Will, serious, attentive, enthusiastic but self-absorbed. The incident is the starting-point for the romance which springs up swiftly between Will and Anna; it also hints at the dissensions which are to trouble their marriage. (Look, for instance, in Chapter VII at the quarrel over the lamb in the stained glass window of Cossethay church or in Chapter VIII at the visit to Lincoln Cathedral.) The interest in churches, in religion, in art and architecture is apparent in the episode. Find at least one further reference to each of these themes elsewhere in the novel.

Linguistically, too, the passage introduces a number of threads which have appeared or will appear in other parts of the novel. Will here is described in animal imagery, as a mole with his 'black, keen, blind head'; he is frequently later described as a cat:

a grinning young tom cat
The lit-up grin, the cat-grin
a young black cat

Find some more examples and list them yourself. Will is also described here as having 'golden-brown, quick, steady eyes, like a bird's, like a hawk's'. Find examples from other parts of the book which use bird imagery to describe Will. Likewise the theme of light and dark appears here, Will being aligned with darkness, when he is compared with an animal that lives 'in the darkness under the leaves' and Anna with light as she sits in church 'amid illumination, illumination and luminous shadow all around her, her soul very bright'. Again find further examples. What about the use made here of both flowers and flower imagery? Is there anything else you would wish to comment on?

You have probably collected enough material by now to write an essay on 'Discuss the scene in which Will Brangwen first visits Marsh Farm and suggest its relevance to the book as a whole'. Take care not to retell the story! Here is an answer to a similar essay on one of the scenes from Ursula's childhood:

Choose any scene from Ursula's childhood and discuss the part it plays in the novel as a whole

---

This essay will discuss the incident in which Ursula tramples over Will's seed-bed and angers him. It is a very short scene, yet it is typical of many other scenes from Ursula's childhood. It begins with Ursula's delight in her childish play and her lack of thought about adult affairs. What child understands the tender loving care which has gone into the making of a seed-bed or, understanding, realises that even tiny footprints will violate its perfection?

Two aspects of Ursula's character are illuminated by this scene. First, we see her thoughtless impetuosity; she runs across the seed-bed in the same spirit as she later gives her necklace to the bargeman's baby; when she is older she learns to control her impulsive actions to some extent, for she endures torments at the Brinsley Street school before she finally canes Vernon Williams. We also see her hurt and vulnerable as disillusion breaks in upon her. This childish disillusion with her father is mirrored in a succession of disillusionments which follow – with church, with religion, with education and with love. The other principal character in this scene is Will who is obsessed by passionate love and by passionate self-absorption. He has tried to dominate Anna but his will has failed against her; here we see his desire to dominate his daughter fail in the face of her unresponsive resistance.

The scenes both of Anna's and of Ursula's childhood display a deep understanding of childhood and are frequently very moving. Lawrence is perhaps at his most successful in such scenes and the emotions of the child are skilfully reproduced for the reader. The extremes of love and hate in Will's attitude to the child leave her in a state of such uncertainty that a sense of unreality develops in her so that she allows nothing outside herself to have power over her: 'She cut off her childish soul from memory, so that the pain, and the insult should not be real'. When she grows into adolescence she goes through a period of religious fervour which comes to an end as she begins to suspect that the 'Sunday world [is] not real' (Chapter XI). This conviction is followed by a comment which links up with the scene discussed in this essay, for we are told, 'She hated herself, she wanted to trample on herself, destroy herself', just when Will reproves her for treading across his seed-bed we learn that 'Her vulnerable little soul was flayed and trampled'.

There is not a great deal of imagery in this passage, though the ideas of chaos and destruction are carried over from the description of the seed-bed to the state of Ursula's childish soul 'clinched in the silent, hidden misery of childhood'. The contrast between fire and cold is present too when unreality hardens Ursula 'like a frost' so that Will feels 'a flame of rage go over him' at her apparent indifference. Look at this essay again. Before it was written a plan was made in note form:

PLAN:

(1) Introduction: Choice of scene
                          Setting of scene

(2) Characters: (a) Ursula
                        (b) Will

(*a*) Impetuosity – references to gift of necklace (Chapter XI) and Brinsley Street School (Chapter XIII).

Disillusionment with father – references to other disillusionments – church, religion, education, love.

(*b*) Desire to dominate – a reference to desire to dominate Anna.

(3) Childhood scenes
Lawrence's understanding of childhood; Ursula's sense of unreality – appears later with reference to religion (Chapter XI); Ursula's desire to destroy memory of Will's anger.

Quotations:
'She cut off her childish soul from memory, so that the pain and the insult should not be real.'

. . . the Sunday world was not real.'

'Her vulnerable little soul was flayed and trampled.'

'She hated herself, she wanted to trample on herself, destroy herself.'

(4) Imagery. Not a great deal.

Chaos and destruction.

Fire and cold.

Quotations:
'clinched in the silent, hidden misery of childhood.'

'like a frost.'

'flame of rage.'

The plan itself is, of course, the result of considerable preparation, with constant and close reference to the text.

This final section has been designed, not to save you from working, but to help you to work more efficiently. For this reason you have been constantly urged in these notes to find things out for yourself, to become well acquainted with Lawrence's text and to return to it again and again. Ways of dealing with questions have been suggested and they have required you to return to the novel's text to collect your material. Here is a further list of questions to think about; and three more model answers follow them.

(1) Consider the importance of the part played in the novel by *either* (*a*) Lydia Lensky *or* (*b*) Winifred Inger *or* (*c*) Anton Skrebensky.

(2) Discuss Lawrence's interest in relationships.

(3) Consider the significance of the rainbow symbol in the novel.

(4) What is the most striking feature of Lawrence's style in this novel? Discuss with illustrations.

(5) What makes the novel more than a chronicle history?

(6) Discuss the significance to the whole novel of Chapter I, section I.

(7) To what extent does *The Rainbow* chart the progress of time in the Victorian era?

(8) How significant is Paul Lensky to Lawrence's theme?

(9) Choose an episode which throws light on the character of *either* (*a*) Tom Brangwen (husband of Lydia), (*b*) Will Brangwen or (*c*) Ursula Brangwen. Show how the character is illuminated for the reader.

(10) 'The chapter on Ursula's experiences in Brinsley Street School is self indulgent.' Do you agree?

(11) Examine in detail the final paragraph of Chapter I, 'They were such strangers . . . cover of cloud again' and use it as a starting-point for commenting on Lawrence's style and language in *The Rainbow*.

(12) Can you suggest reasons why Lawrence at one time considered using *The Wedding Ring* as a title?

The model answers which follow are the result of considerable preparation. Before the essay is started, and after an initial thorough reading, the text must be skimmed through, notes taken and quotations jotted down. Then an essay plan must be made on the lines suggested above. Only then is it possible to write a rough draft of the essay. What appears here is a final, more polished piece of work. Once you have read the essays try to work out the original plan for them.

Model answers

Question (1): Consider the importance of the part played by (*b*) Winifred Inger

Winifred Inger is the young schoolteacher with whom Ursula has a brief Lesbian affair and who later marries Ursula's uncle Tom.

Ursula has recently experienced her first passion of love for Anton Skrebensky and he has now returned to the Army and has been posted to South Africa to take part in the Boer War. Ursula is distraught, not because Anton has gone away, but because at first she does not suffer as much as she thinks she should; there is 'a cold imperturbability in her soul' and she feels 'as if some disillusion had frozen upon her' (Chapter XI). It is when she is in this state, her spirit raw and sensitive, that she becomes aware of a very special feeling towards Winifred Inger.

For a full term Ursula dreams and daydreams of Miss Inger and this new love helps her to forget the aching wound of Skrebensky's departure. In Ursula's last term at school the affair develops in that Ursula finds that Winifred reciprocates her interest. It becomes a physical affair with the touch of the teacher's fingers on Ursula's cheek and the following weekend the two go away together to a bungalow on the Soar. As always, Lawrence retreats from being specific; though the language of passion is used suggestively: 'she put her arms round her, and kissed her. And she lifted her in her arms, close . . . Ursula twined her body about her mistress', it is not clear how far the affair really goes, but it is clear that Ursula later suffers a revulsion and wishes to have no more to do with Miss Inger. It is her second disillusionment in love.

Winifred Inger is also the first woman to introduce Ursula to the Women's Movement. *The Rainbow* was being written when Women's Emancipation was very much to the forefront of the times and Ursula is brought into contact with several women who urge her interest in the development of women's freedom. After Winifred, Ursula finds that Maggie Schofield, a fellow-teacher at Brinsley Street School, has a similar interest and later Dorothy Russell, Ursula's college friend, also talks to her on the same theme. Yet there is no point in the novel where we feel that she becomes committed to the Women's Movement.

When Ursula feels that her love for Winifred Inger is beginning to cloy she makes what appears to be a cold-blooded decision to marry Winifred to Tom Brangwen; Ursula, who has previously held a great fondness for her uncle Tom has in some way become disillusioned with him too and we are told, 'She hated her Uncle Tom, she hated Winifred Inger'. The coldness which follows the earlier warmth of love should perhaps prepare us for her rejection of Skrebensky later.

The last we hear of Winifred after her marriage to Tom Brangwen is that she has borne him a child.

Question (2): Discuss Lawrence's interest in relationships

Many different kinds of relationships are presented in *The Rainbow*, the principal ones being those between the sexes, either leading to marriage, as with Tom and Lydia and Will and Anna, or breaking off in complete disillusion as with Ursula and Skrebensky. For Lawrence, a perfect union between the sexes must recognise both singleness and duality in each individual. He shows Tom and Lydia as a couple who at first do not easily come to terms with each other's individuality:

'What am I to remember about you?' said Brangwen.
'I want you to know there is somebody there besides yourself . . . . To you I am nothing . . .'
'You make me feel as if *I* was nothing,' he said.

Because they can talk of their problems they are able to come together in joy, however, and their union is more successful than that of Will and Anna who are unable to come to terms with each other.

Between Ursula and Skrebensky the relationship is an affair of physical passion, but the two have nothing else in common and are unable to satisfy each other spiritually. The affair draws to an inevitable conclusion with disillusion on both sides. Ursula is clearly attracted to the physical in men for she momentarily toys with the idea of marriage to Anthony Schofield who is described as 'strong and well made, with brown, sunny, easy eyes and a face handsomely hewn'. Lawrence refers to one or two other similarly physical relationships, such as that of Tom with the girl in the hotel at Matlock or that of Will with the girl in the Empire at Nottingham; in these two affairs it is again Tom who is able to give himself fully so that both find satisfaction and Will who tries to dominate the girl so that neither is satisfied.

Another relationship which recurs in the book is that between parent and child. This is first referred to when Tom is a boy and we are told that his mother 'admired most' his brother Alfred, but Tom 'was his mother's favourite'. At this stage, however, there is no development of the theme. The most significant parent-child relationships are between Tom and Anna and Will and Ursula. Tom is a kind and understanding step-father and cherishes Anna, comforting her when she is unhappy and providing her with entertainment and amusement on her own terms. It is a delightful relationship and though she has a brief moment of defiance of him when she and Will tell him of their intended marriage, the love between them is close and warm throughout their lives. With Will and Ursula it is different for though he loves her he wishes to dominate her: 'he had a curious craving to frighten her' and thus he jumps into the canal with the infant Ursula clinging to his back or drives the swingboats at the fair until they hang almost perpendicular. This streak of cruelty in him turns Ursula gradually against him so that by the time she has left school she has little feeling left for him and after a quarrel about her going to work we are told, 'She knew she was free – she had broken away from him'.

Finally, Lawrence is concerned in this novel with relationships between two people of the same sex. There is a brief reference in the first chapter to 'an almost classic friendship, David and Jonathan' between Tom Brangwen and a schoolfriend, but most of the other relationships are centred on Ursula. At different times various friendships are referred to – with Ethel, with Maggie Schofield, with Dorothy Russell – which are simple friendships or interchanges of confidence and kindly comfort in moments of difficulty. Only the relationship with Winifred Inger goes beyond that of friendship and Lawrence takes the two through a period of ecstatic passion to final disillusionment.

Question (11): Examine in detail the final paragraph of Chapter I and use it as a starting-point for commenting on Lawrence's style and language in *The Rainbow*

This paragraph follows the proposal of marriage which Tom makes to Lydia. After their moments of peace together there is a sense of dividedness as they part. It is this sense of separation that gives point to the use of the words, 'They were such strangers'. The strangeness, the foreignness that is between them is twofold; Lydia's attraction for Tom is in the very fact that she is from outside, but at the same time the strangeness suggests the individuality of each. Lawrence emphasises these aspects of their relationship by repeating both the word 'strangers' and the word 'foreignness' in a matter of a few lines. The device of repetition is constantly used throughout the novel.

The remainder of the paragraph develops the cosmic imagery which is a feature of this book. A sense of the smallness of man and his concerns is given to us as Tom goes out into the night and the wind blows 'holes . . . into the sky' or blows 'the moonlight . . . about'. The rich and restless vocabulary concentrates on vastness and movement: 'high moon', 'hollow space', 'electric . . . cloud-edges', 'vast disorder', 'flying shapes', 'great brown circling halo', 'scudded', 'teeming and tearing along', 'running', 'plunged'. The cosmic imagery throughout the novel is used in this way in order to add scope and magnitude to the plot; it helps to turn the chronicle of a family into a chronicle of mankind.

Although this is a night scene, words have been carefully chosen which suggest not only the moonlight but the rainbow too, for such phrases as 'liquid-brilliant', 'brown-iridescent cloud-edges', 'a radiance . . . a vapour', 'ragged fumes of light' would fit in well with the description of a rainbow forming in the sky. The passage should be compared with the penultimate paragraph of the book in which Ursula observes the rainbow which brings her release from her despair and hope for the future; the wind, the blowing clouds, the iridescence are all there.

Lawrence frequently uses such heightened, poetic prose, particularly at the ends of chapters. It enables him to give insights into characters which would be difficult to give by more mundane means. Here we move into the uncertainty of Tom's mind, through the wildness of the sky, but his proposal has brought to his spirit a glory, an 'iridescence' which, like the moonlight, will continue to break out in his life.

Part 5

Suggestions for further reading

The text

There is no good annotated text of *The Rainbow*. The most satisfactory texts are those of the edition published by Penguin Books, Harmondsworth, 1949, and the Phoenix edition published by Heinemann, London, 1971.

Other books by D. H. Lawrence

The White Peacock, Heinemann, London, 1911
Sons and Lovers, Heinemann, London, 1913
Women in Love, Martin Secker, London, 1921
Selected Essays, Penguin Books, Harmondsworth, 1950
The Collected Letters of D. H. Lawrence, ed. Harry T. Moore, Heinemann, London, 1962

Life

Personal memoirs
LAWRENCE, ADA AND GELDER, G. STUART: *Young Lorenzo, The Early Life of D. H. Lawrence*, Martin Secker, London, 1932
'E.T.' (JESSIE CHAMBERS): *D. H. Lawrence. A Personal Record*, Jonathan Cape, London, 1935

Biographies

ALDINGTON, RICHARD: *Portrait of a Genius, But . . .* , Heinemann, London, 1950. An understanding and well-written life.
MOORE, HARRY T : *The Intelligent Heart*, Heinemann, London, 1955; revised as *The Priest of Love: A Life of D. H. Lawrence*, Farrar, Strauss and Giroux, New York, 1974

Critical works

ALLDRITT, KEITH: *The Visual Imagination of D. H. Lawrence*, Arnold, London, 1971

HOUGH, GRAHAM: *The Dark Sun*, Duckworth, London, 1956
LEAVIS, F. R.: *D. H. Lawrence, Novelist*, Chatto and Windus, London, 1955
LERNER, LAURENCE: *The Truthtellers: Jane Austen, George Eliot, D. H. Lawrence*, Chatto and Windus, London, 1967
NIVEN, ALASTAIR: *D. H. Lawrence: The Novels*, Cambridge University Press, Cambridge, 1978
SMITH, F. GLOVER: *D. H. Lawrence: The Rainbow*, Arnold's Studies in English Literature, Edward Arnold, London, 1971

The author of these notes

HILDA D. SPEAR was educated at Furzedown College of Education, London, the University of London, and the University of Leicester. She has taught in various schools, colleges of education and universities, including Purdue University, Indiana. She is now a Senior Lecturer in the Department of English, the University of Dundee. Her publications include *Remembering, We Forget* (1979); an annotated edition of *The English Poems of C. S. Calverley* (1974); and *The Poems and Selected Letters of Charles Hamilton Sorley* (1978). She wrote the biographical and bibliographical section of *The Pelican Guide to English Literature V*, and she has published articles on teaching English as well as on R. H. Barham, C. S. Calverley, W. M. Praed, Ford Madox Ford, Wilfred Owen, Isaac Rosenberg and Siegfried Sassoon.

She is also the author of York Notes on Thomas Hardy's *The Mayor of Casterbridge*, Joseph Conrad's *Youth* and *Typhoon*, and William Golding's *The Spire* and *The Inheritors*.